Richard Humble
Stephenson High School

D1708205

Designer	Cooper/West	
Art Director	Charles Matheson	
Series Editor	James McCarter	
Editor	Jenny Mulherin	
Reseacher	John MacClancy	
Consultant	Charles Messenger	
Illustrators	Andy Farmer	
	Rob Shone	

Designed and produced by
Aladdin Books Ltd
70 Old Compton Street
London W1

*First published in the
United States in 1985 by*
Franklin Watts
387 Park Avenue South
New York

ISBN 0 531-10078-2

Library of Congress
Catalog Card No. 85-50514

Printed in Belgium

*The publishers would like to thank the following organizations
and individuals for their help in the preparation of this book:*
Robin Adshead; Mr Alloway, Fleet Headquarters, Northwood,
The BBC Hulton Picture Library; Central Office of Information;
Commander Compton-Hall; Lockheed International
Corporation; McDonnell Douglas Corporation; Ministry of
Defence; Military Archives Research Services (MARS); Newport
News Shipbuilding Ltd, Mr Antony Preston, US Navy Public
Relations Department; Robert van Tol; Whitton Press and special
thanks to Dorchester Typesetting Group.

Photographic Credits.
4/5 DAVA; 8/9 Robin Adshead; 10/11 DAVA, David Higgs;
12/13 David Higgs; 14/15 DAVA; 16/17 David Higgs, Central
Office of Information, DAVA; 18/19 David Higgs, US Navy Photo
Center; 20/21 Central Office of Information, DAVA; 22/23 US
Navy Photo Center, McDonnell Douglas; 24/25 Central Office of
Information, MacClancy Collection; 26/27 Newport News
Shipbuilding, Stuart Guman; 28/29 Lockheed; 30/31 MacClancy
Collection; 34 to 44 Image Press, Robert Hunt Library, US Navy
Photo Center, Whitton Press, MARS, Ministry of Defence, BBC
Hulton Library.

20th CENTURY WEAPONS

SUBMARINES

RICHARD HUMBLE

FRANKLIN WATTS

New York · London · Toronto · Sydney

Introduction

The submarine is one warship dreaded by even the most powerful of the world's navies. Since it first went to war in 1914, the submarine has been able to destroy enemy merchant ships, warships, troopships, and invasion craft. And since their entry into service in the early 1960s, nuclear-powered submarines carrying ballistic missiles armed with thermonuclear warheads have also threatened civilian populations living hundreds of miles inland.

Diesel/electric and nuclear submarines

There are two basic types of submarine. Diesel/electric submarines run on diesel engines when surfaced and switch to electric motors on diving. They are easier and cheaper to build than nuclear submarines, which use the same powertrain – steam turbines "fired" by the heat of a nuclear reactor – whether surfaced or submerged.

A diesel/electric submarine must return to the surface at regular intervals to recharge its batteries from a generator driven by the air-breathing diesels. It can do this running just below the surface, drawing air for the diesels through a hollow tube (known as the "snorkel" or "snort"), but is still vulnerable to enemy surface and air attack.

Nuclear submarines do not have this restriction. They can run thousands of miles submerged, renewing air, distilling water and recharging batteries without having to surface.

Yet diesel/electric submarines, when being hunted, can switch everything off and lie totally silent. Nuclear submarines, whose pumps must keep controlling the nuclear core temperature, cannot do this.

How submarines are classed

Submarines are classed according to how they are powered and what they do. Conventional hunter/killer or "attack" submarines use torpedoes or submarine launched missiles to attack enemy surface ships or submarines. They may also be equipped to lay mines or carry out surveillance.

Diesel/electric attack submarines are coded SS and nuclear-powered attack types SSN. Submarines carrying nuclear missiles are different. They play a "strategic" role in that the missiles that they carry remain a constant threat to any country that first makes use of nuclear weapons. Submarines carrying Cruise missiles are coded SSG or SSGN if nuclear-powered. Nuclear-powered ballistic missile submarines are classed SSBN.

Contents

Above: USS *City of Corpus Christi* of the Los Angeles class

Anatomy of a Submarine

This is HMS *Valiant*, which entered service in July 1966 as Britain's second SSN. Both diesel/electric and nuclear submarines have the same basic structure: a cylindrical pressure hull enclosed by a streamlined outer envelope which contains the ballast tanks.

Inside the pressure hull

The pressure hull is circular in cross-section for maximum strength. It protects crew, engines, equipment, weapons, and stores from underwater pressure, which increase the deeper the submarine dives. Watertight doors, mounted in reinforced bulkheads, convert the submarine's interior into a chain of sealed compartments. If the hull fails under pressure, or (much more likely) is breached by accidental collision or enemy attack, damage and flooding may only be confined to the compartment or compartments involved. If the submarine cannot be saved and the accident occurs in shallow water, the sealed-off compartments at least offer the rest of the crew a chance to escape or be rescued.

The streamlined "sail" or "fin"

Rising above the outer casing, the flattened and streamlined conning-tower is called the "sail" or "fin." It provides a bridge from which the submarine is controlled or "conned" when on the surface. It also houses the upper mountings of the periscopes, through which sea and sky may be visually scanned from beneath the surface. There are usually two periscopes, one for normal surveillance and a smaller one for close-range work. Both are raised and lowered from the control room below. Also mounted on the sail are the radar scanner and communications aerials.

1 Propeller
2 Rudder
3 Hydroplane
4 Main ballast tanks
5 Aft escape hatch
6 Main gearing
7 Motor room
8 Reactor compartment
9 Fin
10 Radio aerial
11 Periscope
12 Control room
13 Senior ratings lounge
14 Forward access hatch
15 Forward hydroplane
16 Torpedo storage area
17 Torpedo tubes
18 Sonar arrays

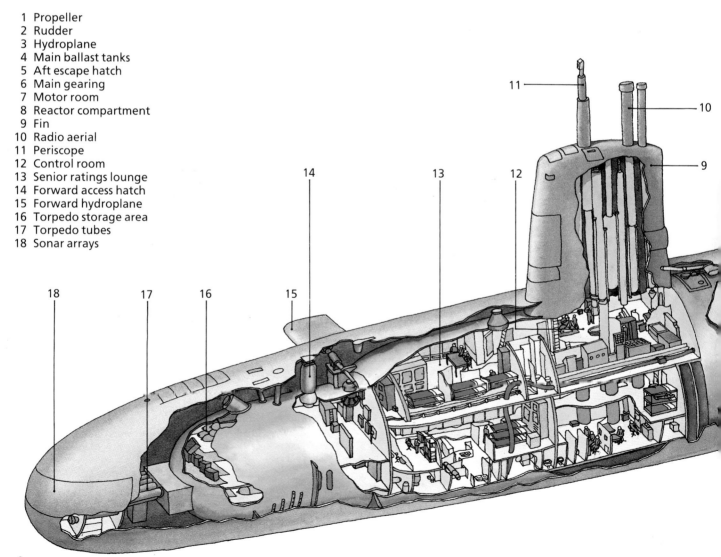

Access and weapons hatches

From the sail, the pressure hull is entered through two stout hatches, which are clamped shut when the submarine dives. Other hatches through the pressure hull permit access to the outer casing, for the loading of supplies and weapons, or for normal access when in harbor. SSBNs have a long double row of hatches astern of the sail, each capping one of the tubes from which the submarine-launched ballistic missiles (SLBMs) are fired.

Hatch-closing drill

Hatches represent the most obvious threat to hull integrity and the safety of the submarine. Any hatch left open when diving, either through human error or communications failure, could easily result in an uncontrolled plunge to the seabed, or to a depth at which the pressure hull would collapse. A painstaking routine of checks and double-checks before diving is invariably followed, making any such accident extremely unlikely.

Torpedo tubes, shafts, and hydroplanes

Apart from hatch openings, the pressure hull must also be pierced to mount the ballast tank vents, the torpedo tubes, shafts, masts, periscopes, rudder spindles, and hydroplanes.

The torpedo tubes launch the main weapons of modern attack submarines. Though some diesel/electrics still carry both bow and stern tubes, the faster, more streamlined SS, SSNs, and SSBNs carry all their tubes in the bow, in groups of four, six or eight. Automatic torpedo reloading gear saves much time and energy.

The shafts transmit the drive from the engines to the screws. Diesel/electrics and most Soviet nuclear submarines have two or more shafts, but all American, British, and French SSNs and SSBNs have a single shaft. Whether mounted on the hull or on the sail, the hydroplanes are pitch controls. Angled up or down, they control the submarine's angle of descent or ascent and keep the submarine at the correct depth when submerged.

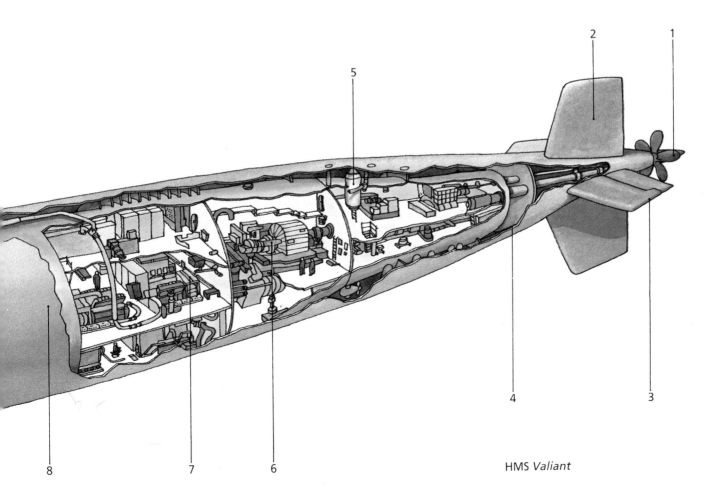

HMS *Valiant*

The Powertrain

Until the end of World War Two, nearly all submarines were faster under diesel power on the surface than under electric power submerged. Speeds underwater seldom exceeded 18 knots, not enough to out-run enemy surface warships.

More power from "Guppying"

The only way to make conventional submarines faster underwater was to lengthen the hull, adding more powerful electric motors and sufficient extra batteries for them. The post-1945 US rebuilding program known as "GUPPY" – Greater Underwater Propulsive Power – involved slicing a submarine in two. A lengthened "power-pack" hull section was then inserted, and the submarine finally reassembled and streamlined. This Guppying greatly increased the service life of submarines as well as their speeds underwater. Some of these Guppied submarines are still in service with the world's smaller navies.

Diesel/electric performance

The finest diesel/electric submarines were the three US Barbels: USS *Barbel*, *Bonefish* and *Blueback*. The last diesel/electric attack submarines built for the US Navy, they were commissioned in 1959. They had fully streamlined "teardrop" hulls and singleshaft drive. They could reach speeds of up to 15 knots on the surface and an impressive 21 knots submerged.

Nuclear reactor, steam turbines

Although some nuclear submarines carry auxiliary diesels and electric motors, their main engines are extremely powerful steam turbines. These turbines are propelled by a nuclear reactor, usually pressurized and water-cooled by electric pumps. There are normally two turbines, delivering a horsepower of 30,000 or more. This means that submerged speeds in the most powerful SSNs are usually in excess of 30 knots.

The basic machinery of SSBNs is much the same as the SSNs: cooled reactor, geared steam turbines, and single shaft. All known Soviet SSBNs have at least two shafts, and some classes have three. Underwater speed is not so important in SSBNs, since they are not attack submarines. Even so, the reported horsepower of the huge US Ohio class Trident SSBNs is 60,000. Submerged speeds for SSBNs average 25-30 knots.

Core life and cruising range

The SSN's enormous speed superiority over the diesel/electric is matched by its longer life in operation. Even the first US SSNs, commissioned in 1955-59, could steam over 192,000km (120,000 miles) before their first nuclear core change. A diesel/electric of later date may be capable of only 14,400km (9,000 miles) or less on diesels without refueling. The core life of the new US Los Angeles SSN is estimated at ten years.

Engine room of the nuclear-powered HMS *Conquerer*

Generating electricity

As well as driving the propeller, a submarine's engines provide electricity for the vessel. Steam from the reactor or from the diesel engines passes into the turbogenerator and drives turbines which in turn generate electricity, just as in an ordinary power station. With crews of 70 to 100 men, a lot of electricity is required for such mundane tasks as heating, lighting and cooking, as well as for powering the many electronic systems on board a modern submarine. There are also battery-generated sources of electricity, for use in an emergency, or when the vessel is under "silent running" to avoid enemy detection.

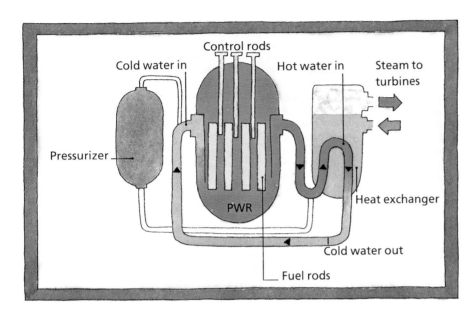

Control rods

Cold water in

Hot water in

Steam to turbines

Pressurizer

PWR

Heat exchanger

Cold water out

Fuel rods

A nuclear submarine has a pressurized water reactor (PWR). Inside the reactor core are uranium fuel rods. These undergo nuclear fission – the uranium atoms break up and release large amounts of energy. The control rods modify the rate of fission – when lowered they absorb uranium atoms to slow the reaction down. Water under great pressure passes from the pressurizer through the reactor core, where it becomes super-heated. It then passes to the heat exchanger where a second water source produces steam to drive the submarine's turbines.

Steam from the reactor drives powerful turbines, although some is also used to generate electricity in the turbogenerator, to power the submarine's electrical systems. The drive passes through reduction gears to the main shaft – some submarines have two shafts for greater efficiency. The clutch on a nuclear submarine also enables the switch from nuclear power to back-up diesels or electric motors to be made. The drive finally passes through the electric motor immediately astern, to reach the propeller.

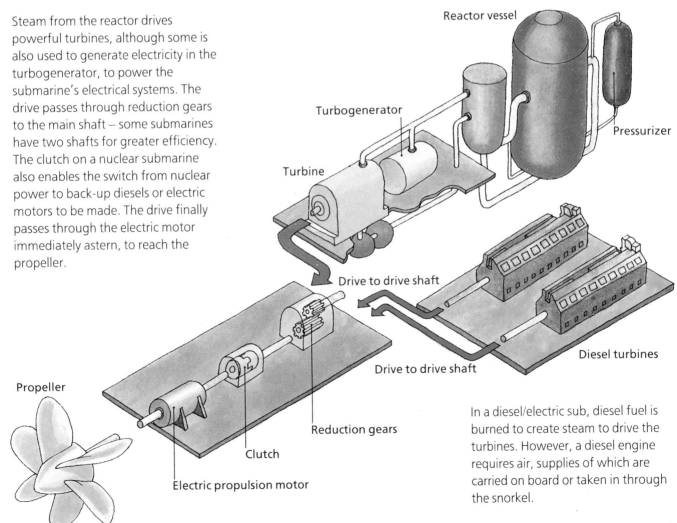

Reactor vessel

Turbogenerator

Pressurizer

Turbine

Diesel turbines

Drive to drive shaft

Drive to drive shaft

Propeller

Reduction gears

Clutch

Electric propulsion motor

In a diesel/electric sub, diesel fuel is burned to create steam to drive the turbines. However, a diesel engine requires air, supplies of which are carried on board or taken in through the snorkel.

Diving and Steering

Like any other ship, a surfaced submarine displaces its own weight of water and it has a natural tendency to float. Diving and returning to the surface involve first cancelling this tendency to float, then restoring it. The positive buoyancy maintained on the surface is changed to negative buoyancy in order to dive, and this negative buoyancy must be reduced to a state of neutral buoyancy as soon as possible to stop the submarine from plunging past the depth required. To do this, the submarine's ballast tanks are flooded with seawater when diving, and the seawater is blown out with compressed air to return to the surface.

A surfacing nuclear-powered Los Angeles class submarine

Flooding the ballast tanks

The flooding and emptying of the ballast tanks, which are open to the sea at the bottom, is controlled by valve-like vents along the top of the tanks. To dive, the vents are opened and permit seawater to rush into the tanks from below, pushing out the air. The replacement of air by seawater in the ballast tanks reduces positive buoyancy and enables the submarine to submerge with the aid of the hydroplanes. In nuclear submarines with "teardrop" hulls and sail-mounted hydroplanes the dive is assisted by the downward pressure of the bow wave, which rests on top of the bow. Submarines can submerge vertically when stopped, but nearly every dive commences with the submarine under way.

The vital trim

Once the ballast tanks are fully flooded, negative buoyancy cannot be replaced by neutral or positive buoyancy, by blowing the tanks empty, until the vents have been shut. For the submarine to remain stable when submerged, it must displace just its own weight of water. It must also be kept balanced, neither heavy forward or light aft, or vice versa. This stable condition is called the trim, and without it the submarine cannot be properly controlled or maneuvered. Many factors affect the submarine's buoyancy. For example, as stores and fuel are used up, the submarine becomes lighter and neutral buoyancy has to be regained. This must be taken into account in order to achieve and maintain trim.

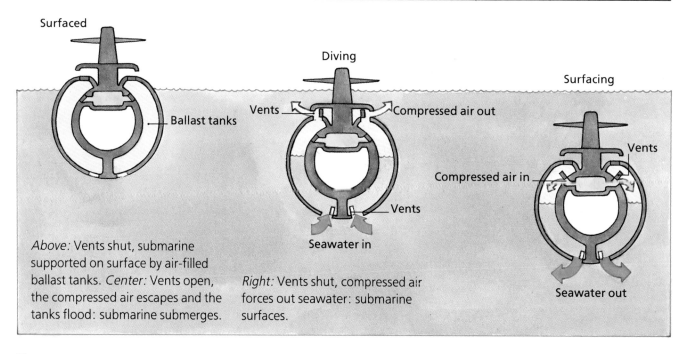

Above: Vents shut, submarine supported on surface by air-filled ballast tanks. *Center:* Vents open, the compressed air escapes and the tanks flood: submarine submerges.

Right: Vents shut, compressed air forces out seawater: submarine surfaces.

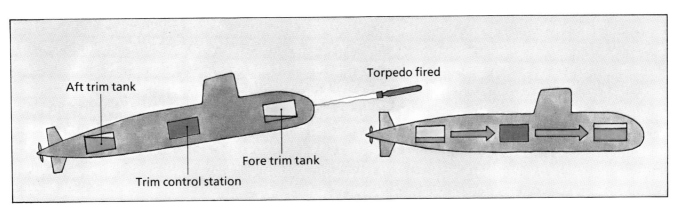

Aft trim tank

Torpedo fired

Trim control station

Fore trim tank

Changes in displacement

A submarine's displacement is constantly changing, as water, fuel, stores and weapons are consumed. There may also be a changing amount of water in the bilge, due to variations in seepage through the shaft, rudder or hydroplane controls. In diesel/electrics, fuel consumption is countered by leaving the fuel tanks open to the sea. This permits seawater to enter the tanks from below as the fuel is drawn off above. The diesel oil floats on top of the rising seawater in the tanks, with no mixing of the two or contamination of the fuel; but the net result is to leave the submarine heavier.

Role of the trim tanks

After diving, an untrimmed submarine may be briefly held stable by the hydroplanes, if the submarine is able to maintain a reasonable speed. But trim is properly maintained by auxiliary ballast tanks inside the pressure hull, distributed along the centerline. Trim is maintained by pumping water fore and aft between these trim tanks.

The trim tanks keep the submarine on an even keel. Here the launch of a torpedo makes the submarine lighter at the bow. This is countered by pumping water forward from the trim tank at the stern.

Performance and steering

If the surface trim is kept too light, diving can be dangerously prolonged in an emergency; if too heavy, the submarine can become unstable. A submerged and correctly trimmed submarine has two main controls: the rudder for yaw (side-to-side turning) and the hydroplanes for pitch (rise and descent).

Circling for advantage

At speeds of over 30 knots, a submerged nuclear submarine can take up several miles of sea, while slower diesel/electric submarines naturally have a tighter turning circle when submerged. The nuclear submarine's speed advantage is of less value when two submerged submarines locate each other and then maneuver to gain "end-on" attacking advantage.

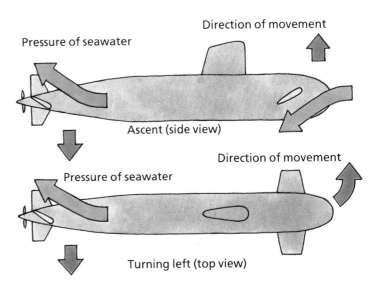

Pressure of seawater

Direction of movement

Ascent (side view)

Pressure of seawater

Direction of movement

Turning left (top view)

At the helm

The helmsmen see a view of the submarine's course, shown on a TV monitor (above). The main controls are the hydroplanes and rudder. The hydroplanes pitch to enable the submarine to move up or down (top right). The rudder gives side-to-side yaw when the sub is surfaced or submerged.

Navigation

The basis of all marine navigation is establishing a regular, accurate fix of the ship's position. This is expressed as a combination of latitude (the number of degrees north or south of the Equator) and of longitude (the number of degrees east or west of the Greenwich Meridian).

Celestial navigation and dead reckoning

Even in the nuclear era, navigating a submarine can use the same ancient principles of celestial navigation as a surface ship does. By day or night, celestial navigation starts by taking a sight from the sun, moon, or stars. This is then checked against tables of known celestial movements in order to get the true position. The constant need of diesel/ electrics to surface for battery charging has always provided a natural opportunity to obtain a celestial sight. But heavy cloud, especially on a dark night, often makes the taking of such sights impossible.

Without accurate sights, the navigator out of sight of land has to fall back on dead reckoning (DR). This is best described as an assumed position based on courses and speeds followed since the last accurate fix. Dead reckoning fixes must also take into account the effects of winds, currents, and tides.

Coastal navigation

In normal peacetime service a submarine, like any other ship, can use radar, and global radio systems such as Consol, Decca Navigator, Loran, and Omega when navigating inshore waters. Looking to wartime conditions, however, total reliance on such systems is impossible. Radar cannot be used because the signals transmitted by the submarine would instantly reveal its position. Nor does a country at war leave even its lighthouses in normal service, let alone international navigation systems, for the benefit of patrolling enemy submarines. Coastal navigation must therefore be used within sight of a hostile coast, with sightings taken through the periscope.

In coastal navigation the most prominent visible landmarks are used: towers, tall buildings, masts, distinctive hills, cliff faces, or rock formations. These provide a fix plotted on the chart from intersecting compass bearings.

When only one landmark is visible, the "running fix" is used. The navigator takes a bearing from the landmark, allows the submarine to run a known distance, then takes a second bearing to get the line of position. The actual fix is calculated by adding the drift factor since the taking of the first bearing.

Checking course: the navigation officer plotting course on a chart.

Computerized navigation

While the navigations officer must have all the traditional methods of navigation at his command, he also has highly sophisticated electronic equipment to aid him. One of the most important of these is the Ship's Inertial Navigation System – usually known as SINS.

How SINS works

The SINS system has no need for any external reference points in order to plot the submarine's changes of course. Instead, it takes the starting point of the voyage as its reference point and gives a continuous computer read-out of the submarine's position.

The system is based on an arrangement of gyroscopes and devices called accelerometers, mounted on a stable base. There are three gyros in all, each with an accelerometer attached. One gyro points east, one north and the third toward the meridian. The accelerometers measure any acceleration of the vessel in these directions. By knowing the northerly and easterly accelerations, the computer can calculate the distance and direction traveled by the submarine. SINS is so accurate that its readings are correct to within 200m (656 ft) after a submerged voyage of over 60,000km (37,280 miles).

Display consoles give instant information update

Satellite fixes

Despite the accuracy of SINS, occasional position checks are made for back-up and verification. Rapid mid-ocean checks can be obtained by orbiting communications satellites. These allow the submarine, showing no more than a slim radio aerial to make an instant check on its position, and submerge again in seconds.

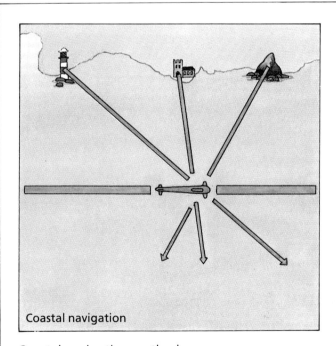

Coastal navigation

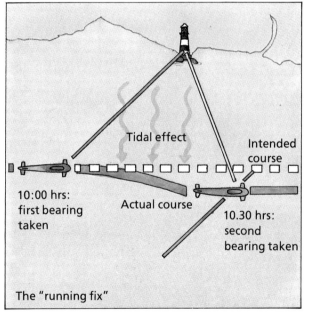

The "running fix"

Coastal navigation methods

In coastal waters, traditional navigational techniques are often used still. If there are three prominent landmarks, an accurate fix can be obtained by taking bearings and plotting these on a chart (above). When only one landmark can be distinguished, a *running fix* is made (above). After the first bearing is taken, the submarine sails for a given time. Then, a second bearing gives the new position reached, thus giving the effects of tide or current that cause the submarine to travel off its intended course.

Communications

All submarines, whether diesel/electric or nuclear, have to maintain regular radio communications with their base. They may also need to make contact with friendly sea and air forces. But this can put the submarine in constant danger. Fear of the enemy "listening in" and decoding messages to and from submarines has been greatly reduced by high-speed scrambled transmissions. But the fact is that a transmitting submarine gives away its position. The enemy is able to scan the different frequencies, and so detect and locate the bearing of the signal being transmitted.

Location by "Huff-Duff"

A vital British device against German U-boats in the Battle of the Atlantic (1940-1943) was High Frequency Direction Finder – HF/DF, or "Huff-Duff." HF/DF enabled allied ships to detect signaling U-boats within seconds of starting to transmit. One surface ship with HF/DF could determine the U-boat's bearing. Two or more ships, able to obtain an intersection of bearings, could determine the U-boat's range. In the 1980s, HF/DF is still a great threat to a submarine's survival, and one of the biggest problems in the field of submarine communications.

Whip aerials and buoys

A submarine's chances of escaping HF/DF detection can certainly be helped by remaining submerged during transmission. This is best carried out either at periscope depth showing no more than a whip aerial, or by floating a radio buoy to the surface. Transmission is kept as short as possible. Then the submarine takes off from the position at which the signal is sent.

Here nuclear submarines obviously are better than diesel/electrics, with their far higher submerged speeds. But it is often impossible for a submarine to get far enough away to escape – especially in battle conditions and if the enemy's speed of reaction is quick.

Communication by satellite

Orbiting communications satellites (COMSATs) enable submarines to "bounce" high-speed transmissions via space to their base. COMSAT signaling drastically reduces the time it takes to

Soviet F class attack submarine alongside a Kashin class destroyer

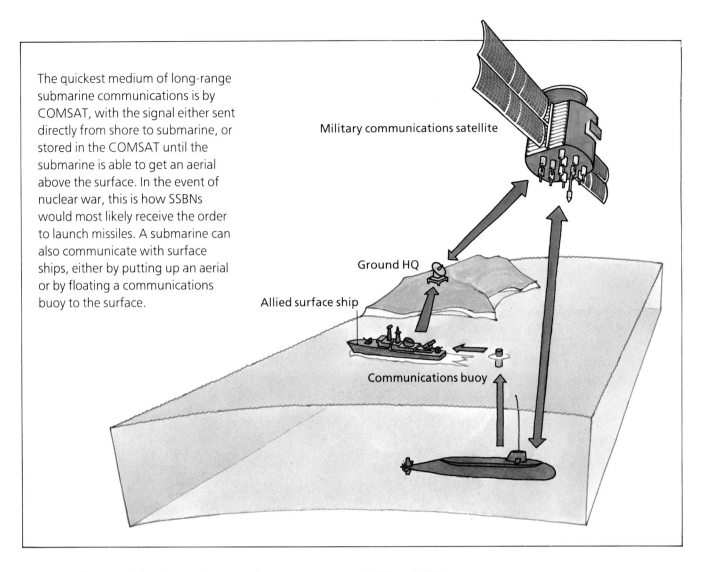

The quickest medium of long-range submarine communications is by COMSAT, with the signal either sent directly from shore to submarine, or stored in the COMSAT until the submarine is able to get an aerial above the surface. In the event of nuclear war, this is how SSBNs would most likely receive the order to launch missiles. A submarine can also communicate with surface ships, either by putting up an aerial or by floating a communications buoy to the surface.

Military communications satellite

Ground HQ

Allied surface ship

Communications buoy

pass a radio signal. It also makes signals more secure from enemy interception. For signals going the other way, from base to submarine, COMSATs have a message "store" which a surfacing submarine can instantly pick up.

The use of COMSAT signaling grows every year. Over 70 percent of all US military messages are already passed by COMSAT. These satellites are launched into geosynchronous orbits. This means that they move "with" the spin of the Earth and they stay in the same sky. Because of this, there is no loss of signal in the area each is intended to cover and they are able to pass messages in "real time," with little or no delays caused by distance.

VLF and ELF

A great deal of research has gone into ways of transmitting signals direct to submerged submarines. This is particularly important with SSBNs. Ordinary radio transmissions cannot penetrate water. For this, Very Low Frequency (VLF) or Extremely Low Frequency (ELF), which can penetrate the ocean to a limited depth, are required, and the submarine must trail a receiver behind it while submerged. Although some success has been achieved, transmitters need enormous amounts of power and have to be housed in giant buildings by the sea. This makes them easy targets for a "first strike" by enemy missiles.

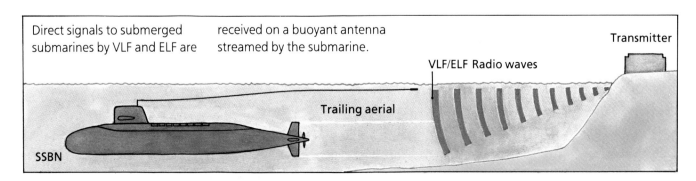

Direct signals to submerged submarines by VLF and ELF are received on a buoyant antenna streamed by the submarine.

Transmitter

VLF/ELF Radio waves

Trailing aerial

SSBN

The Crew's Roles

The size of a submarine's crew or complement always depends on the submarine's own size, type and role, as well as the complexity of its power and weapons systems.

The SS of the 1980s, which is bigger and far more complex than the World War Two type, usually has a complement of 7-8 officers and 55-70 other ranks. This makes totals of 77 in the US's Barbel class, 62 in the Soviet's Tango class, and 54 in the smaller French Agosta class.

Repair being carried out on the hull

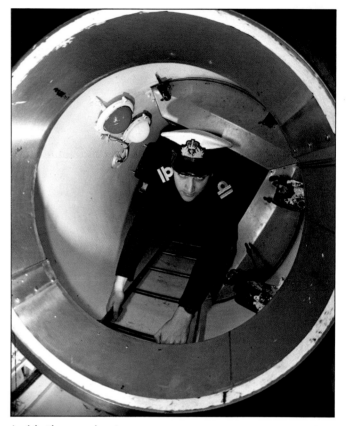

Inside the conning tower

Nuclear submarine crews

Nuclear submarines have much bigger crews than diesel/electric SS. The British Oberon class SS has a complement of 69; the US Los Angeles class SSN has a crew of 127, comprising 12 officers and 115 enlisted men. SSBNs, with their missiles to be maintained, usually have about 30 more crew members than SSNs. To reduce the strain on crews, SSBNs have two crews (called Red and Gold in the US Navy, Port and Starboard in the UK). While one is at sea, the second rests ashore.

The Captain and his "Exec"

Though always referred to as the Captain, the commanding officer of a submarine is usually a Commander, Lieutenant-Commander or even Lieutenant in actual rank. The same applies to the second-in-command: the First Lieutenant or Executive Officer (Exec). One of the "Exec's" traditional duties is to supervise the submarine's trim when submerged. But the "Exec" is also responsible for the efficient organization of the submarine's crew, for routine discipline and morale, and for the submarine's general state of readiness.

Heads of department

Under the Captain and "Exec" come the submarine's departmental heads. Even in the smallest diesel/electric, these have always included a Navigating Officer, Engineer Officer (or Chief Petty Officer), and a Weapons Officer. Some diesel/electrics, as well as all SSNs and SSBNs, now have a Medical Officer. Mine-hunting, communications, radar, sonar, and electronic countermeasures (ECM) also usually have separate heads of departments. The aim in all departments is maximum efficiency and readiness as a single ship's company.

Watches and conditions of readiness

The work of a submarine on patrol is performed in a succession of spells of duty known as watches. These vary according to the condition of readiness, which relates to circumstances outside the submarine. If it is patrolling off a dangerous coast, or navigating under the Arctic pack ice, or encountering surface warships or submarines from rival powers the condition of readiness is raised. When the submarine is in safer waters, the condition of readiness is lowered.

Weapons control room

Torpedo room

Monitoring the air scrubbers

Routine on board

There is always an air of alertness on board a patrolling submarine. The photographs on this page show some of the crew's routine duties. These range from practice weapons drill (above left and above right), to checking that all the submarine's other systems – such as the air purification unit – are in good working order (left). The photograph below gives a good indication of the size of a modern submarine's crew – in this case the crew of a US Los Angeles class SSN.

Basic crew duties

Even when in home waters, routine duties must still be carried out. The engine-room team must be ready to respond instantly to orders from the control room for more or less speed. When the submarine has submerged, the planesmen at the hydroplane controls maintain the submarine's required depth, while other crewmen at the pump stations shift ballast between the trim tanks.

When the submarine is at periscope depth there is a radar watch as well as "eyeball" scanning, through the periscope, by the Captain or officer of the watch. A sonar watch checks for the presence of other submarines, while vertical fathometers monitor the depth in shallow waters, and the rise and fall of the "ice ceiling" when the submarine is navigating under Arctic pack ice.

Crews take part in naval exercises on many patrols so that battle tactics and weapons systems can be tested under realistic conditions. Attack submarines can use discarded vessels as targets for their missiles and torpedoes. But SSBNs must also go through procedures for firing their weapons and crews regularly rehearse the drill sequence laid down for firing their weapons.

Crew on deck at launch of Los Angeles class submarine

Life on Board

The modern submarine of the 1980s is big, clean, dry, and in general well suited to keeping men alert and healthy on long voyages, even though they are often in alien and dangerous environments.

Space and cleanliness
Nowadays, all crew members have their own bunk space and locker, while senior ratings and officers have cabins. Both on watch and off watch there is far more comfort than was ever possible in pre-1945 submarines. This also applies to laundry and personal washing facilities.

"Scrubbed" air, "quiet" colors
Headaches and sickness due to foul air during long submerged periods have also been eliminated. Fresh sea air can be funneled through the "snorkel" when the submarine is running at periscope depth but it is no longer vital. A modern submarine can distill its own water and electrolyze its own oxygen direct from seawater. Mechanical "scrubbers" clean carbon dioxide and humidity from the air, then recirculate it. Heaters and air conditioners keep the temperature at a comfortable level. Even the carefully varied color schemes within the submarine are important. The attractive yet "quiet" colors have been chosen by experts because they are relaxing for crew members and are less likely to cause stress.

Waste and sewage disposal
When submerged for long periods, submarine crews cannot easily dispose of the ship's rubbish by packing it in weighted sacks and dropping it over the side. Another way – the pressurized ejection of rubbish and sewage – may be detected by sound detectors. Waste disposal equipment and large sanitation tanks are now fitted in most submarines in order to control this problem.

Relaxation off watch
The greatest care and attention is paid to encouraging relaxation when off watch. In nuclear submarines, there are generous recreation spaces for all ranks. And there are also libraries and even movies on board.

Preparing food in the galley

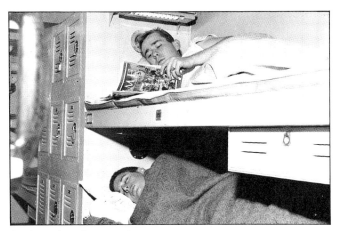

Ratings sleeping quarters

Wash-room

The officers' mess on board a British submarine

The ratings' mess can also be converted into a temporary cinema

Submarine Sensors

Without sensor equipment a submerged submarine would be deaf and blind. It would be unable to detect approaching enemies or to navigate safely in busy or restricted waters.

The first submarine sensor was the periscope. It gives the submarine's commander an all round visual picture of the world above the surface. Its lens can be swiveled vertically to scan the sky as well as the sea. This is a vital need, because of aircraft on anti-submarine warfare patrol and the danger of a surprise air attack when running just below the surface.

The periscope operator (if not the Captain, the officer of the watch) normally has the choice of at least two lenses. There is a standard lens for routine scanning of sea and sky, and a high-definition lens when "close-up" vision is required. When carefully exposed at low speeds, a periscope is almost impossible to spot except in the calmest seas.

"Quiet" and "noisy" submarines

These Hydrophonic Effects (HE) give every type and class of submarine a distinctive "sound print" which can be recorded on tape and analyzed by an expert operator, or referred to a computer data bank. The type of submarine detected can thus be quickly identified – and hence its likely role, performance, and range of weapons can also be determined.

In HE terms, submarines are either "quiet" or "noisy;" and it goes without saying that the ideal is the quieter, the better. Quietness is achieved by improved streamlining and also by installing more efficient machinery. But diesel/electrics are silent when stopped and "switched off." Nuclear submarines have to keep their reactor-cooling electric pumps and turbogenerators running at all times, even when stopped. This means that they always run the risk of hydrophonic effects being given out.

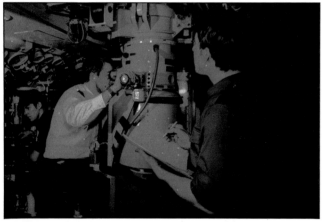

Looking through the periscope

The "eye" of radar

The periscope has its electronic equivalent in radar. Radar's revolving beam detects the approach of surface ships and aircraft in poor visibility or bad weather. But like all electronic sensors, radar has one disadvantage. It is easily detected by enemy receivers.

Underwater sound detection: the hydrophone

The next sensor to be used was the hydrophone. First used in action in 1914-1918, this detects the sounds given out by nearby surface ships and submarines – churning screws, engines, the passage of the hull through the water, and sounds inside the hull.

Sonar is by far the most important submarine sensor. The main concentration of sonar transducer/ receivers is in the bow, to locate obstacles in the submarine's path; but an all round sonar "vision" is required to locate other submarines in both the vertical and horizontal planes. Sonar is also used to detect mines, take depth soundings from the seabed, and trace the contours of surface ice when navigating under the Arctic pack.

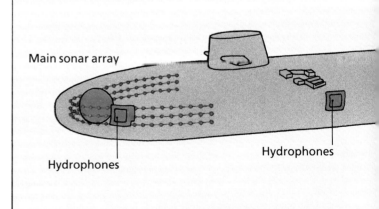

Main sonar array

Hydrophones

Hydrophones

Active and passive sonar

The hydrophone's "listening ear" is the passive element of sonar, the most important submarine sensor. Sonar – "Sound Navigation and Ranging" – originally was developed as an anti-submarine device. The name sonar has replaced the original asdic since 1945. Asdic stood for the "Allied-Submarine Detection Investigation Committee." This was an Anglo-French research team which solved the problem of detecting submerged submarines on the eve of World War Two.

Passive sonar only listens for HE and enemy sonar sounds, and it is useless when there are none to hear. But active sonar sends out a regular sonic pulse, or "ping," which bounces back as an echo when it hits a solid surface. This ping can actually be heard from inside the submarine that is being detected. Sonar operators are trained to tell the difference between whales or schools of fish, and genuine submarine echoes.

Apart from detecting the bearing and range of nearby submarines, active sonar is also used to hunt mines. It can also scan and help map the irregularities of the seabed and the fluctuating ceiling of overhead pack ice.

Identifying sonar signature after a contact

Now sonar enables nuclear submarines to navigate under Arctic pack ice, amid the ever-changing natural hazards in the narrow seaway between ice "ceiling" and seabed. In this constricted environment the biggest danger comes from above, in the form of "ice keels." These are floes tilted on edge by the constantly moving Arctic pack ice, creating vertical ice walls which could cause fatal damage if not located in time.

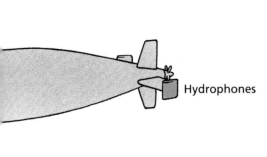

Hydrophones

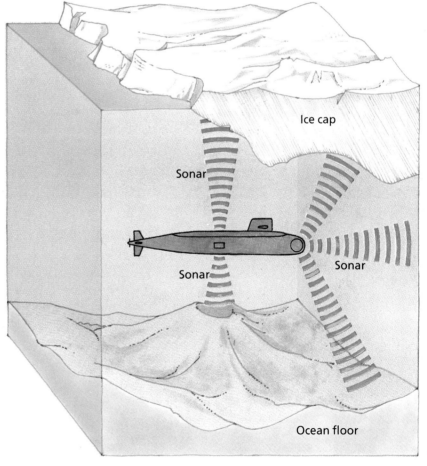

Ice cap

Sonar

Sonar

Sonar

Ocean floor

SSBN Weapons

The main function of the SSBN is to discourage the outbreak of nuclear war by acting as a launch-platform for submarine-launched ballistic missiles (SLBMs). Compared with land-based inter-continental ballistic missiles (ICBMs), SLBMs are lighter and possibly less accurate. Even so, the latest SLBMs can match older ICBMs in range (about 6,500km (4,000 miles)) and time from launch to target (about 30 minutes). This means that a missile fired from beneath the middle of the Atlantic Ocean could reach a wide range of targets deep within Europe, the United States or the Soviet Union.

Likely targets

Cities are the likeliest SLBM targets. By the time that SSBNs received the order to attack, enemy airfields and missile sites could have been wiped out in the first land-based missile (ICBM) attacks.

Alternatively, enemy sites could have fired their last ICBMs and not be worth attacking. So the real threat of the SLBM is to make sure that enemies know that no matter how much damage they cause with their ballistic missiles, their civilian populations can still suffer mass destruction by SLBMs.

How SLBMs are fired

As it is launched from the submarine, an SLBM is shot to the surface slightly off the vertical, to prevent it from falling back on the SSBN if it malfunctions. As it breaks the surface the main rocket motor ignites, and gyros guide it into its pre-calculated target trajectory.

Elaborate precautions are taken to prevent any accidental firing of an SLBM. Two officers, each with their own key, are needed to install the firing

Inside the missile tube

switch, and safeguards are taken to prevent any unauthorized person who might go berserk and try to sabotage or fire the missiles.

Missile tubes and multiple warheads

Nearly all the SSBNs carry 16 SLBM tubes. But what really matters is not the number of SLBMs per submarine, but the number of warheads per SLBM. From 1970 onwards the US Poseidon missile replaced the "first generation" Polaris SLBM. Poseidon carried a pack of 10 to 15 independently targetable warheads (MIRV), ready to separate on to individual targets after arrival in enemy airspace. The latest Trident SLBM is expected to be armed with 14 to 20 warheads. The huge new US Ohio class SSBNs will carry 24 of these each, a minimum of 336 targets for one submarine.

Missile tubes on an Ohio class SSBN

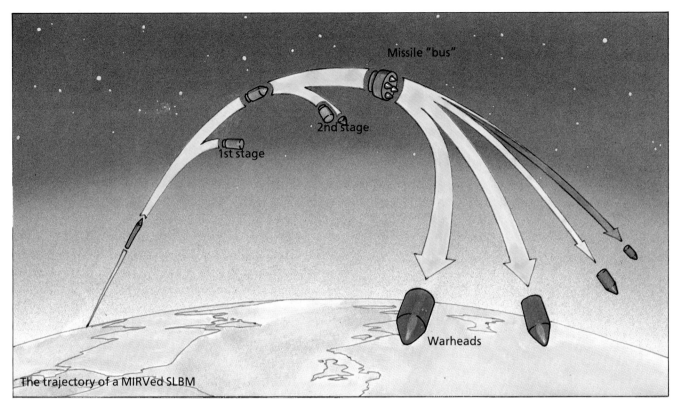

The trajectory of a MIRVed SLBM

Trident missile

The potential destructive capability of the SLBM has been vastly increased by the advent of MIRV – Multiple Independently targetable Re-entry Vehicles. The first MIRVed SLBM was the US Poseidon. Poseidon has ten to fourteen warheads, each of which can be directed to a different target. The missile has two stages to launch it into orbit above the Earth. here, the "bus" carrying the warheads separates from the last stage. The warheads are then released in sequence, and each has a pre-set guidance unit to fly to its target. The targets can be different cities hundreds of miles apart, or the warheads can fall as a cluster on a single area – vastly increasing the destructive effect against such "hard" targets as protected ICBM launch sites. With MIRVing, the world's nuclear armories must be calculated in terms of the number of warheads rather than missiles. For example, the 31 SSBNs of the Lafayette class carry from 5000 to 7000 warheads.

Low-flying Cruise missiles

Apart from SLBMs, the other category of submarine-launched strategic missiles is that carried by the SSGs and SSGNs: Cruise missiles.

Submarine-launched Cruise missiles (SLCMs) were first deployed in the 1950s by the Soviet Union. Unlike SLBMs, they can be fitted with high-explosive warheads for conventional use against surface warships. Most Cruise missiles, whose flight is powered by a "turbofan" jet engine, must be launched on the surface, but the new US Tomahawk can be launched submerged, by torpedo tube. It then breaks surface and extends its wings to fly below enemy radar cover, guided by a "ground-hugging" automatic guidance system. The Tomahawk missile has an effective range of about 2,420km (1,500 miles).

Tomahawk Cruise missile

Attack Submarines

In both World Wars the main submarine weapons were the torpedo and the deck gun. The torpedo was used for attacks when submerged and the deck gun for action on the surface. But after 1945 the development of submarines altered. Their traditional role on the surface was abandoned and the deck gun was given up. At the same time, there were radical design changes in the torpedo, which became the main weapon of the new-look, high-performance attack submarine.

Still in use: the basic torpedo

The least complicated torpedo type, used in both World Wars, is still widely used. This has a simple guidance system based on a gyroscope, which keeps it running at a fixed depth on a dead straight line. When it is driven by compressed air and diesel fuel, the cheapest propellant, it leaves a distinctive track of bubbles in its wake. If these are sighted in time by alert lookouts, these bubbles can give a target warship the chance to steer out of the path of an oncoming torpedo.

The first homing torpedoes

The first torpedoes, which made some attempt to seek out a target, were developed for the German U-boat fleet. This torpedo, called the "zigzag runner," was designed for use at long range. Its pre-set zigzag course increased the chances of finding a target when fired into a convoy of merchant ships.

Another homing torpedo, the German acoustic torpedo, was designed to home in on the target's propeller noises. But its guidance system was primitive. It was unable to concentrate on genuine target noises and to ignore decoys. A simple countermeasure was soon found in the noise-emitting "foxer." This could confuse the guidance system with nothing more complicated than two lengths of metal pipe, towed astern, to clatter in the wake. But the German acoustic torpedo of 1943 was the forerunner of torpedoes to come. Far more sophisticated countermeasures are required for the submarine weapons of the 1980s.

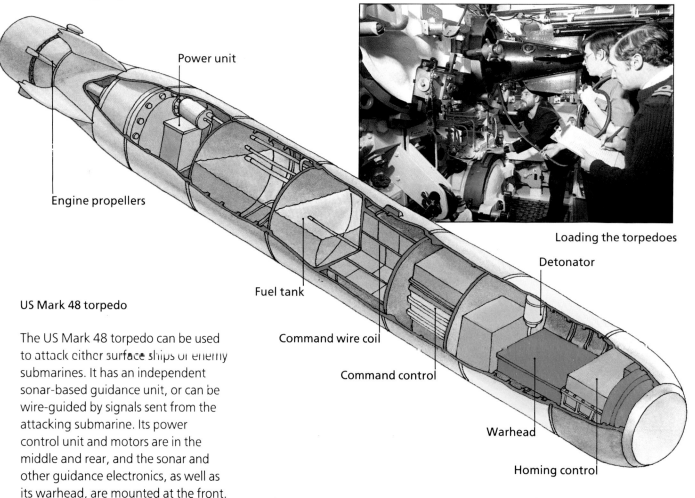

Loading the torpedoes

US Mark 48 torpedo

The US Mark 48 torpedo can be used to attack either surface ships or enemy submarines. It has an independent sonar-based guidance unit, or can be wire-guided by signals sent from the attacking submarine. Its power control unit and motors are in the middle and rear, and the sonar and other guidance electronics, as well as its warhead, are mounted at the front.

Wire guidance and pattern running

The "cleverest" modern torpedoes have a choice of several guidance systems. Torpedoes with acoustic guidance may also have wire guidance. In this system the torpedo is guided to the target by signals relayed through a wire which is unreeled from the torpedo and tube after launch. Pattern running is a program which sends the torpedo on a methodical "hunt" for its quarry. If it misses the first time, it heads straight in to attack once the target has been found again.

However, the only torpedo attack yet made by an SSN, HMS *Conqueror*'s sinking of *General Belgrano* off the Falklands in May 1982, used none of these complex and immensely costly modern weapons. It was sunk by two "old faithful" Mk8 torpedoes which were of pre-Second World War design.

Submarine-launched missiles

Apart from torpedoes, submarines can launch two types of missile. The first type, such as Harpoon or Tomahawk, is an anti-ship missile. It breaks surface and, flying at a low level, is guided straight to its target. The second type, such as Subroc, is an anti-submarine missile. It breaks surface, flies to the target area, and then plunges back into the water again, to surprise and destroy submarine targets.

But in the 1980s not even the fastest, most sophisticated torpedo in service can be guaranteed to catch nuclear submarines running fast and deep. Among the most difficult targets to reach are submarines speeding at over 30 knots at depths of more than 305m (1,000 ft).

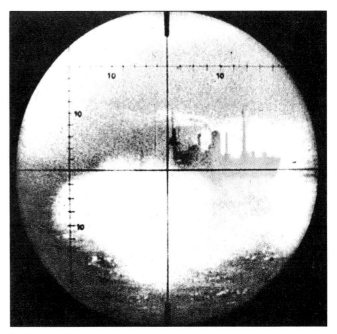

Periscope view

Minelaying by submarine

Mines have always been as deadly to submarines as to surface ships, and the submarine has often been used as a minelayer. Nowadays this is usually done by the diesel/electrics. Minelaying is a dangerous business. Even the discharge of small mines through torpedo tubes can be detected by enemy sonar. And in calm weather the discharge may actually be seen. Like torpedoes, mines can be detonated in a number of ways. One is physical contact with the mine, others are acoustic contact and detonation by the victim's magnetic field.

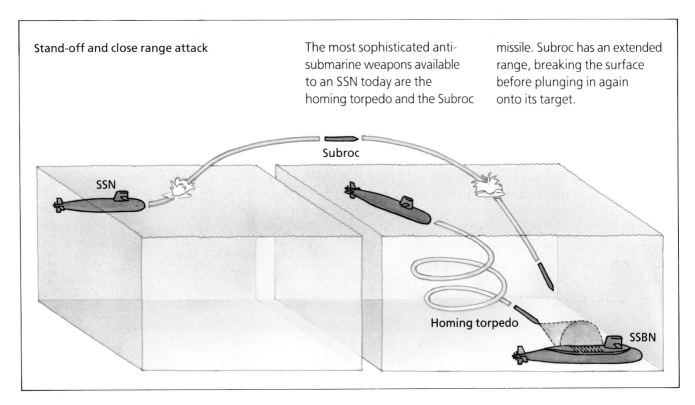

Stand-off and close range attack

The most sophisticated anti-submarine weapons available to an SSN today are the homing torpedo and the Subroc missile. Subroc has an extended range, breaking the surface before plunging in again onto its target.

SSN

Subroc

Homing torpedo

SSBN

Submarine Tactics

Los Angeles class submarine

The submarine became a decisive naval weapon long before it was given the ability to destroy enemy cities with SLBMs. Both World Wars proved that submarines could stop the flow of vital war supplies by sea. This nearly made it impossible for Britain to survive, and made Japan's defeat inevitable in 1945. It is uncertain how these experiences apply to a Third World War. But the modern Soviet Navy certainly has far more submarines than Germany ever used in 1914-18 or in 1939-45. In a Third World War, this big Soviet submarine fleet would pose a very great threat to the NATO navies – and also to NATO supply convoys.

Peacetime patrolling

Apart from SSBNs, submarine patrolling in peacetime is aimed at showing strength to likely enemies. In most instances, patrolling takes place in areas where the other side would least like their rivals to be in the event of war. In the case of the superpowers, this means close to the exits from Soviet home waters (by NATO submarines) and far out beneath the high seas, especially the Norwegian Sea and Atlantic (by Soviet submarines). The movements of these submarines are constantly monitored by opposing chains of Soviet and NATO sound-detectors. These are deployed across the most obvious strategic bottlenecks in northern waters, on the seabed of the continental shelf.

War of the "hunter-killers"

In the event of a major war there would probably be an early duel between the "hunter-killer" SSNs of the hostile navies. It is likely that these battles would extend under the Arctic ice, since submarine encounters are already frequent there. Submarines maneuvering to attack each other would make great use of electronic countermeasures (ECM) to jam the other's sensors.

Combat is likely to take place more quickly in the shallow and restricted waters near continental land masses, because here SSNs cannot make the fullest use of their ability to go fast and deep.

SSN attack

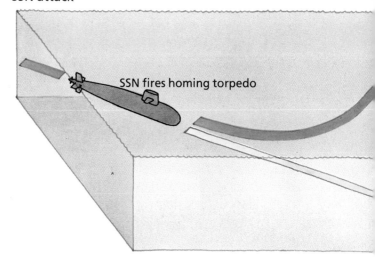

SSN fires homing torpedo

Targets: SSBNs and enemy surface forces

A major and early target would be each side's SSBNs. Detecting SSBNs is already a familiar feature of naval exercises in peacetime. Fears that SSBNs could be found quickly and destroyed could possibly mean that the war's "nuclear threshold" would be crossed quite early on. It is likely that SSBNs would be ordered to fire their SLBMs while they were still able to do so.

Other targets for submarines would be carrier battle groups and also anti-submarine surface forces. These would most probably be attacked with torpedoes, air-to-surface missiles, or Cruise missiles.

The Falklands experience, 1982

One of the biggest worries of the British Task Force in April-June 1982 was Argentina's small fleet of four diesel/electrics. But the Argentine navy had much more to fear from the far-ranging British SSNs. After the sinking of the old cruiser *General Belgrano* by the British on May 2, the Argentine fleet stayed in its mainland bases for the rest of the war. This is the most recent and striking example of just how effective the submarine can be in naval warfare as a tactical deterrent.

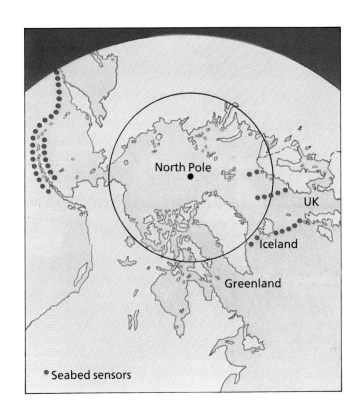

● Seabed sensors

Monitoring Polar waters

The Arctic Ocean is a major area of submarine activity. Seabed sensors cover all major routes in and out.

Once enemy craft have been detected, a number of weapons can be used to destroy them. Here an SSN identifies an enemy submarine and destroys it by homing torpedo. The SSN then moves closer to the other enemy target – the surface warship on the right – and comes to periscope depth to fire a Harpoon surface-to-surface missile. This has a range of up to 109 km (68 miles) and flies at wave-top level beneath enemy radar to destroy its target. The hunter-killer SSN is protected by various anti-submarine defenses such as minefields and roving helicopters dunking sonar probes.

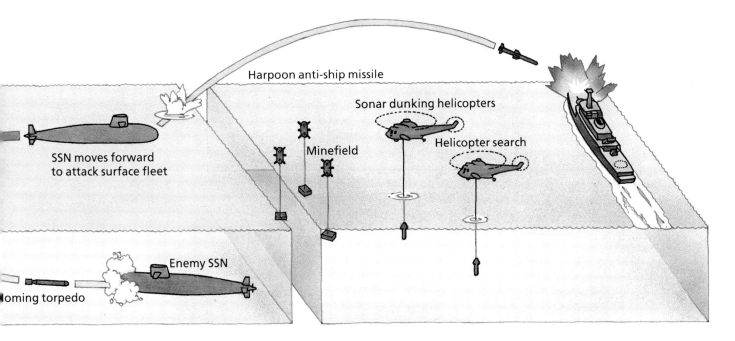

Harpoon anti-ship missile

Sonar dunking helicopters

SSN moves forward to attack surface fleet

Minefield

Helicopter search

Enemy SSN

Homing torpedo

Combat: Submarine Detection

The diagram below shows how the basic techniques of anti-submarine warfare (ASW) work. Some are designed for use in the shallower waters of the continental shelves, others for ocean depths.

Magnetic Anomaly Detector (MAD)

MAD is a sensor designed for fixed wing aircraft carrying out anti-submarine patrols. Before MAD, aircraft on patrol could only hope to catch submarines on the surface, and they had to attack before the quarry could dive and escape. MAD enables aircraft to detect submerged or "snorting" submarines and attack without alerting the vessel by a sonar pulse. MAD does this by spotting irregularities in the Earth's magnetic field. The bigger the submarine, the bigger the irregularity (or anomaly) created by its mass.

Helicopter search

Another latecomer to ASW was the helicopter. This is used for "dunking" sonar buoys into the sea. If the helicopter hears nothing, it moves to another area and searches there. Using this technique a helicopter can quickly search a wide area of sea on a single hunt. Sonar "dunking" by helicopters operating from the shore can also provide surface ships with an outer ring of anti-submarine security and can thus help warships to keep close formation. This means that they offer greater protection to each other and to any carrier they may be guarding. As the Falklands War proved in 1982, this is of particular importance when enemy air attacks are likely. If these take place it is vital for ships to support each other with "pooled" missile and gun fire-power.

Towed sonar equipment

Sonar in surface ships is inevitably affected by the ship's own noises, particularly at high speeds. Apart from reducing speed to a crawl – and this is useless when hunting modern submarines – one way of reducing this interference is to tow a sonar device in

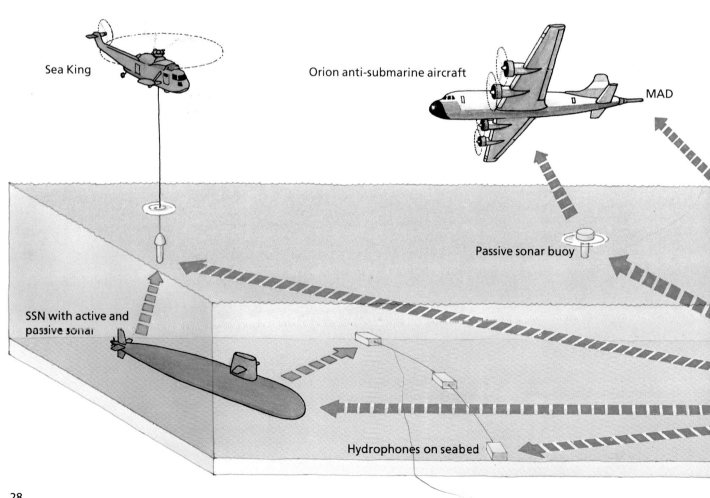

Sea King

Orion anti-submarine aircraft

MAD

Passive sonar buoy

SSN with active and passive sonar

Hydrophones on seabed

P3 Orion anti-submarine patrol accompanied by a destroyer

the ship's wake, making sure it is well astern of the churning screws. Towed sonar devices make deep-water probes and are designed to be used at a wide range of speeds. Their disadvantage is that they hamper movement in an emergency or if a surprise attack takes place.

Seabed hydrophones
These listening devices were used to monitor the underwater approaches to ports and anchorages as far back as the First World War. They are still important because they can provide a warning of any submarines pushing into inshore waters.

This diagram shows the basic search techniques in anti-submarine warfare (ASW). Here the main objective is the SSBN on the right. Arrayed against it, on the left, is a chain of hydrophones and a Sea King helicopter carrying out a roving search by dunking sonar buoys. A long-range patrol aircraft is equipped with MAD (located in the aircraft's tail) and drops sonobuoys carrying both passive and active sonar. The surface destroyer on the right has sonar equipment along its hull and also tows sonar equipment behind it. The attack SSN on the far left is also an effective search weapon as it constantly scans the ocean with both active and passive sonar.

Active sonar array destroyer

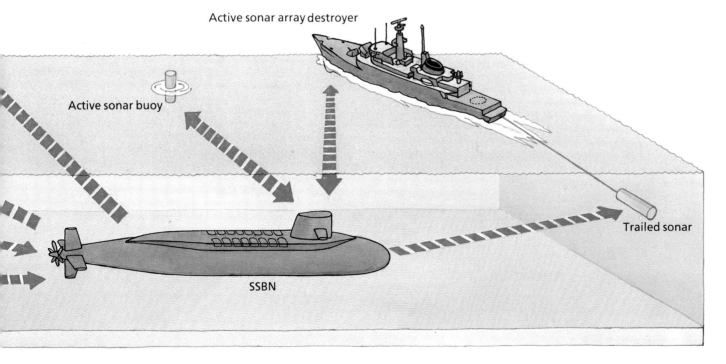

Active sonar buoy

Trailed sonar

SSBN

Anti-Submarine Warfare

This diagram shows the main ways submarines can attack in the 1980s. A great deal has changed since World War Two, when Allied submarines sank only 2.7 percent of all the 785 German U-boats lost. The powerful "hunter-killer" SSNs would certainly raise that percentage if a prolonged submarine war occurred in the future.

Nuclear minefields

In 1939-45, mines destroyed 3.5 percent of the German U-boats lost. This is another percentage likely to rise. Nuclear minefields, as well as conventional mines, must now be reckoned with the naval defenses of the superpowers. Nuclear minefields are designed to wipe out submarines which could be pushing too close to continental shores. Any submarine would have to be on the very edge of an undersea nuclear explosion in order to survive the enormous power of such a blast.

Importance of shipborne helicopters

In the Second World War, surface ships and shore-based aircraft were responsible for the loss of over 62 percent of U-boats. Shipborne aircraft, in the days before helicopters, sank only 5.5 percent. In a future submarine war, shipborne helicopters "dunking" sonar would play a very important role while shore-based aircraft would probably be less vital.

The "sharp end" of anti-submarine warfare is the attack which follows search and detection. In this example the target is the SSBN on the right of the picture. The destroyer on the left has fired an Ikara, a small radio-controlled aircraft launched from surface ships which, like Subroc and Harpoon, flies to the target area before plunging to attack as a homing torpedo on the SSBN. The SSN on the left has the option of attacking with homing torpedoes or, if so fitted, with Subroc. The helicopter has dropped a Stingray homing torpedo, while the elderly destroyer on the right still relies on the traditional depth charges which explode at pre-set depths. Like the minefield on the far right, depth charges and missiles are packed with powerful explosives and a direct hit is not necessary in order to cripple a submarine. However, if fitted with nuclear charges, these weapons could produce a devastating "sledgehammer" effect.

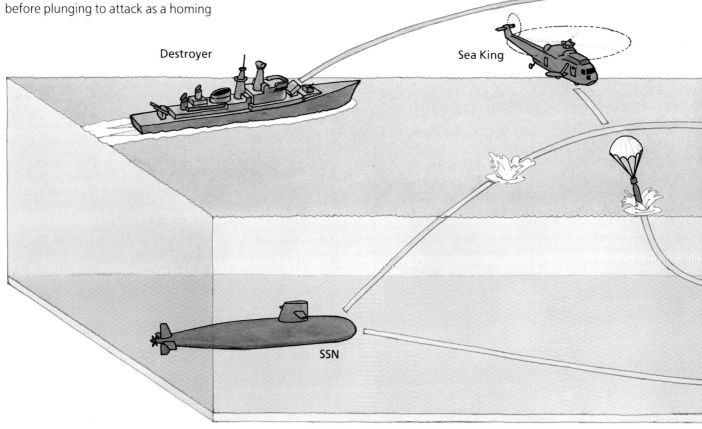

Destroyer

Sea King

SSN

Anti-submarine weapons

The traditional anti-submarine weapon is the depth charge. It was used in both World Wars and, like the torpedo, is still widely used today. The depth charge is a non-guided bomb, fitted with a pressure fuse pre-set to explode at the target submarine's estimated depth. Other more sophisticated weapons, which have hunting devices, can be parachuted or dropped into the sea to track down their quarry. But the cheapest anti-submarine weapon used by surface ships is still the depth charge.

Using nuclear weapons?

A hunted submarine's best chance of escape is to outstrip pursuing weapons, and free-falling depth charges, by going fast and deep. With a good start, its chances of escape are good. The "sledgehammer" technique against such submarines before they can escape is to use nuclear depth charges and nuclear minefields. If, in the future, a major submarine war takes place such weapons could well be used.

Ship-launched Ikara missile

Westland Lynx helicopter armed with Stingray missiles

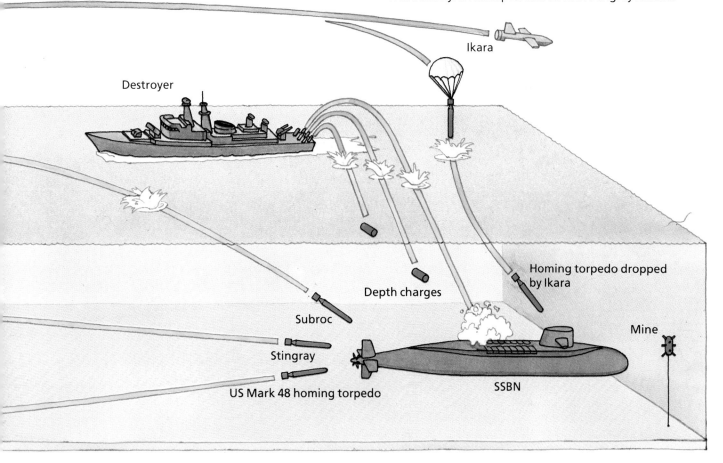

Ikara

Destroyer

Homing torpedo dropped by Ikara

Depth charges

Subroc

Stingray

Mine

US Mark 48 homing torpedo

SSBN

The Future

Thirty years after the first nuclear-powered voyage, by USS *Nautilus*, it is natural to feel that submarines have reached the limits of their development. This certainly applies to the giant SSBNs of the 1980s: the American Ohios and Soviet Typhoons. These ships are much larger and infinitely more destructive than most aircraft carriers of World War Two.

And yet the Trident missile is no more the "ultimate" submarine weapon than the first mark of Polaris turned out to be. The size of a submarine and its range of weapons are important but its development in the future is more likely to be influenced by the demands of actual combat.

Continued use of SS

It seems safe to say that diesel/electrics will always retain two important advantages over SSNs. These are silence (being able to "switch off") and a much tighter turning circle when they maneuver to attack. Attempts will certainly continue to make all submarines "quieter," to give them wider and longer-ranging sensors, and better ECM to upset enemy sensors.

Improving ASW techniques

In ASW, there will be greater reliance on active sonar detection to counter improved submarine "quietness." Satellite communications will certainly be extended. So, too, will submarine detection by satellite, using infrared (IR) scanners to spot the heated water which is constantly "sweated" into the sea from reactor cooling systems.

Submarine technology will probably lead to vessels capable of hiding at even greater ocean depths, and efforts will continue to develop an effective high-speed, deep-diving, hunting torpedo as an alternative to nuclear weapons.

Latest Soviet Typhoon class SSBN

Submarines: History and Development

Although regarded as a 20th century weapon, the fighting submarine was an idea which had been under steady development for some 300 years before 1900. There had always been obvious advantages in producing a submersible warship which could escape the crushing fire-power of surface warships, and attack them from below the surface. But the submarine story is an excellent example of invention being frustrated by lack of technology – especially in engineering and propulsion.

It was not until the 1890s that a truly effective power source was developed by the American, John Holland, using the new internal combustion engine for surface propulsion and electricity for submerged propulsion. By 1900, Holland-type submarines formed the prototype submarine fleets of the world's major navies.

The final step was taken between 1908 and 1914 with the adoption of the diesel engine for surface propulsion, with its much less dangerous fuel. This replaced the previous gasoline, heavy-oil, and steam engines used in the "first generation" submarines of the early 1900s.

The First World War (1914-18)

By 1914 about 400 submarines were in service in 16 navies, roughly half of them British and French; but controversy raged over their combat value in an age which confidently expected decisive fleet actions between Dreadnought battleships and battle cruisers, fought at over 20 knots. But within six months all doubts had been dispelled by the sinking of the first Allied warships by the torpedoes of German *unterseeboote* or "U-boats." Fear of submarine torpedo attack by U-boats paralyzed battle fleet movements throughout the war, most notably in the battles of the Dogger Bank (1915) and Jutland (1916). Both sides also used submarines as minelayers.

But the power of the submarine was most powerfully demonstrated in commerce destruction. Germany carried out unrestricted U-boat assaults on the Allied merchant fleets in 1917, which brought Britain to the brink of outright defeat before the belated adoption of defensive convoys turned the tide. The German U-boat "ace," Arnauld de la Perière, sank an incredible total of 195 Allied ships and became the most successful submariner of all time. Most of his kills were scored in surface gun actions, far more economical than torpedo attacks.

The Second World War (1939-45)

In the Second World War the most successful submarine navies were those which had abandoned the notion of using submarines as an extension of the surface fleet. German U-boat attacks again brought Britain to the verge of defeat in 1940-43; but in the Pacific (1941-45) American submarines succeeded where the U-boats had failed in the Atlantic, destroying 5.5 of the 6 million tons of merchant shipping with which Japan had gone to war, and one out of every three Japanese warships was sunk.

By the end of the Second World War, anti-submarine warfare had been transformed by the integration of air search and attack, and by the dramatic extension of electronic aids (most notably sonar, radar, HF/DF radiolocation, and MAD).

The nuclear era (1945-85)

By 1945 the desire to counter the new anti-submarine devices with a new generation of high-speed submarines, free of the need to surface repeatedly, had already been seen. Though diesel/electric types will always retain an important role, the transformation of the submarine was completed with the development of nuclear attack and strategic missile submarines from the middle 1950s.

Holland VIII (*1900, USA*)
The Holland VIII was the first submarine class to enter naval service, and the model for all "first-generation" submarine fleets. Armed with a single bow 45.7cm (18 in) torpedo tube, these Holland submarines had a crew of seven.

U-15

U-1 (*1906, Germany*)
The German Navy's first U-boat was only completed after three similar craft were ordered by the Russian Navy in 1904. She displaced 242 tonnes (238 tons) (to the 109 tonnes (107 tons) of the 1900 Hollands) and had a crew of 19. Like her 18 successors, the Körting main engines of *U-1* were fueled by heavy oil, giving off dense clouds of smoke.

U-15 (*1912, Germany*)
Completed only six years after *U-1*, *U-15* belonged to the second last class of Körting heavy-oil U-boats built before the First World War. Only three more were being built before the switch to diesels with *U-19*. The vital statistics of *U-15* reflect the rapid pace of submarine development in the first decade of the 20th century. *U-15*'s displacement was 525 tonnes (516 tons) to the 242 tonnes (238 tons) of *U-1*. She was 15.5m (51 ft) longer, armed with two bow and two stern torpedo tubes instead of *U-1*'s single bow tube, and mounted a 51mm (2 in) gun for surface action.

E class (*1913, Britain*)
This was the most numerous class of British submarines in the First World War, 56 being completed between 1913 and 1916. They were big boats for their day with a displacement of 670.5 tonnes (660 tons) and a crew of 30. They had five torpedo tubes arranged as two bow, two beam, one stern. E-21/56 were built as minelayers, with their beam torpedo tubes being replaced by mine tubes. They could carry 20 mines. A 12-pounder gun was carried for gun actions on the surface.

Clorinde class (*1913, France*)
The ten boats of this class were completed during 1913-14. They were of "medium" type with 416.5 tonnes (410 tons) displacement, a crew of 27, and eight torpedo tubes. They were also the first French submarines to be powered by diesel engines, the previous types having been given a wide variety of steam, oil and gasoline engines for surface propulsion.

U-35 (*1914, Germany*)
This was the most successful commerce-raiding submarine of all time. Under the command of the "ace of aces" Lothar Arnauld de la Perière, *U-35* sank 453,855 tonnes (446,708 tons) (195 ships) between November 1915 and March 1918. Her total "catch" for the whole of the First World War was 544,474 tonnes (535,900 tons) (224 ships). *U-35* belonged to the U-31 class (*U-31/41*); she and her ten sister ships were all completed in 1914-15. They displaced 696 tonnes (685 tons), and had crews of between 32 and 39. Their armament consisted of four torpedo tubes, and either one or two 86mm (3.4 in) guns, or a single 104mm (4.1 in) gun. The U-31 class was powered by diesel engines.

UB-1 class (*1915, Germany*)
The UB-1 class was the first class of German coastal U-boat. They were lightweights of 129 tonnes (127 tons), with crews of 14. The first 17 UBs had heavy-oil engines, but the other 138 all had diesels, developing 60-120 hp which gave them a speed of about 6 knots. There were only two bow torpedoes and no guns, though later UBs were fitted with single 86mm (3.4 in) or 51mm (2 in) guns. Four of the UB-1 class were converted to lay mines from four chutes, each holding two mines. Many of these small submarines were dismantled and shipped south by rail to Pula (Yugoslavia) on the Adriatic where they were reassembled for service in the Mediterranean.

British E class

Clorinde class

J class (1916, Britain)
The six submarines of this class were an ambitious development of the earlier G class, Britain's first ocean-going submarines. Driven by three screws, the seven Js which carried crews of 44, were the biggest and fastest submarines of their time (displacing 1,230 tonnes (1,210 tons) and with a speed of 19.5 knots), being surpassed only by the massive submarine cruisers which also appeared in 1916. The Js also had a notably imaginative torpedo armament of four bow and two beam tubes.

Tigr (1916, Russia)
The clumsy design of Tigr is a good example of how many First World War submarine designers tried, mistakenly, to cram in as many surface warship features as possible. In Tigr's case this took the form of treating her as a submersible torpedo-boat, rather than as a submarine with the supreme advantage of being able to attack submerged. Hence the mounting of the eight torpedo tubes in the deck casing, and the addition of heavy deck guns. A further disadvantage was that low-powered diesels were used, stripped from river monitoring boats because of mounting production difficulties.

O class (1917, USA)
After setting the pace for the rest of the world with the small Holland

class at the turn of the century, US submarine design did little for over a decade. A determined isolationist policy denied the US Navy of any clear-cut objectives which would have helped define the type of submarine most needed. By the time the USA entered into the war in 1917, however, the experience of the combatant navies had helped produce the sound US O class submarines. There were 16 boats in the class, eight of which survived to serve as training boats throughout the Second World War (1939-1945) before finally being scrapped in 1946. They were 508 tonnes (500 tons) displacement with a crew of 32. The armament consisted of four bow torpedo tubes and a 12mrn (.50 in) machine gun.

U-151 class (1917, Germany)
These huge submarines of 1,536 tonnes (1,512 tons) began life as submarine merchant ships which were designed to beat the British blockade during the First World War. The first of them, Deutschland (later U-155) made two successful voyages to the USA in 1916. She and her six sister ships were converted as submarine cruisers for long-range raiding in the mid-Atlantic Ocean after the start of unrestricted submarine warfare in early 1917. They had at least one heavy gun (150mm (5.9 in) or 104mm (4.1 in)), and more often two, plus two bow torpedo tubes. Like many early big submarines they were under-powered, their diesels delivering only 800 hp. The crew was 56.

K class (1917, Britain)
These incredible ships were submarine cruisers of 1,913 tonnes (1,883 tons), with crews of 50 to 60. Their most notable feature was steam turbine propulsion giving top surfaced speeds of 24 knots. As they were, the bows were too fine and tended to drive under at high speeds. The K ships were, therefore, rebuilt with distinctive high, bulbous bows. They were designed to carry four bow torpedo tubes and another firing across the beam. Two other tubes were mounted in the superstructure, but most of these were removed during the bow refit, along with one of the original two 102mm (4 in) guns. A 76mm (3 in) anti-aircraft gun was also carried to counter the threat of enemy air attack.

British K class

Surcourf

Requin class (*1926, France*)

Nine submarines of this class were ordered for the French navy in 1922-23, and they were completed in 1926-27. They used the diesel/electric powertrain whose value had been realized by experiences during the First World War. They were designed as ocean-going submarines with four bow and two stern 53.3cm (21 in) torpedo tubes. Their most interesting feature was two trainable mounts for twin torpedo tubes, outside the pressure hull but under the deck hull, fore and aft of the conning tower. The Requins also carried the, by now, standard deck gun 99mm (3.9 in).

Balilla class (*1928, Italy*)

The four submarines of this class were the first big submarines built for the Italian Navy after the First World War. They were laid down in 1925 and the last was completed in

Balilla

April 1929. Their displacement was 1,390 tonnes (1,368 tons) and the usual crew was 78. The Balilla class was specially designed for deep diving, with unusually tough hull construction and a novel hull design. The ballast tanks were resited and the engines positioned much further forward than usual. The armament consisted of six 53.3cm (21 in) torpedo tubes, a 119mm (4.7 in) deck gun, and four 15mm (0.6 in) machine guns. *Balilla*, the name-ship of the class, was fitted for laying four mines, but this facility was abandoned for the other three.

RO 60 class (*1928, Japan*)

Japanese submarine design between the World Wars (1919-1939) was aimed at finding the type best suited to what was later to prove an ill-founded strategy. This was that submarines should operate in squadrons in support of the surface fleet, instead of being freed for offensive operations of their own. The nine RO 60 boats laid down in 1922-23 were improved versions of the RO 57 class, which had been based on the Vickers design for the British L class submarine. The displacement was 1,000 tonnes (988 tons), with a crew of 60. The armament was six 53.3cm (21 in) bow torpedo tubes, a 76mm (3 in) deck gun and a single machine gun.

Surcouf (*1934, France*)

Until the giant Japanese I-400 class of 1944, *Surcouf* had the distinction of being the world's biggest submarine. With over 3,048 tonnes (3,000 tons) displacement, she was 110m (361 ft) long, with a crew of 150. *Surcouf* was perhaps the weirdest offshoot of the 1922 Washington Naval Treaty, that sought to limit warship building following the First World War. She was conceived as a long-range submarine cruiser which could not only be armed with the heaviest cruiser guns permitted by the Treaty which was 203.3mm (8 in) but she could also carry a small seaplane in a watertight hangar. As well as her twin 203.3mm (8 in) gun turret, *Surcouf* was armed with four bow torpedo tubes and another eight in twin mountings aft. She proved useless either as a commerce-raider or as a conventional attack submarine and her career as a Free French Allied warship (1940-42) was not a happy one. *Surcouf* s loss in February 1942 is shrouded in mystery.

K class (*1936, Russia*)

As the USSR's Navy remained little more than a coastal defence force until after the Second World War, it always relied heavily on submarines. The K class consisted of 13 unusually ambitious large submarines, completed from 1936 onwards. They were designed for an ocean-going capacity with 1,412 tonnes (1,390 tons) displacement and a large torpedo armament of no less than ten 53.3cm (21 in) tubes, plus two 99mm (3.9 in) guns and two 45mm (1.8 in) anti-aircraft guns.

Type IIB (*1936, Germany*)

When Germany embarked on the construction of a new U-boat fleet (forbidden by the 1919 Treaty of Versailles), its first boats were small coastal types (IA, IIA, IIB). Their design was based on the UB-II class of the First World War. By the outbreak of the Second World War in September 1939, 30 of Germany's 57 U-boats were Type IIs, and 18 of those 30 were Type IIB. They displaced 283 tonnes (279 tons) and had a crew of 25. The armament was three 53.3cm (21 in) bow torpedo tubes and a 20mm (0.8 in) anti-aircraft gun. In its limited minelaying capacity, the Type IIB could carry eight mines instead of the normal six torpedoes.

Adua class (*1936, Italy*)

Italy went to war in June 1940 with 100 submarines in commission and about 80 ready for immediate service. This was a far more powerful force than the still-modest German U-boat fleet, which in September 1939 had only 22 ocean-going U-boats. The Adua class which reached completion between 1936 and 1939 was fairly representative with 17 boats in all. It was the most numerous class of Italian submarine completed between the World Wars. The later Adua class submarines were considerably modified but the average displacement was 677 tonnes (667 tons), and with a crew of 45. The armament consisted of four bow and two stern 53.3cm (21 in) torpedo tubes, plus a 99mm (3.9 in) gun and from two to four 13.2mm machine guns. Fortunately for the British, the Italians made poor use of their submarine fleet, which suffered heavy losses; only one Adua submarine survived the war. *Sciré*, however, served as the "mother ship" for a number of human torpedo raids which sank or damaged British ships, notably in Gibraltar in 1940 and in December 1941 when the battleships *Queen Elizabeth* and *Valiant* were sunk at Alexandria. *Sciré* was eventually sunk off Haifa in August 1942.

British U class

Russian K class

U class (*1938, Britain*)

These small boats (550 tonnes (540 tons), and complement of 33) were conceived as training submarines, but the demands of the Second World War gave them a highly successful role in coastal and confined waters – especially in the Mediterranean. Their small size made them much more difficult to detect than the larger British S and T class submarines in service at the time.

1-16 class (*1938, Japan*)

These five submarines were the first Japanese class laid down after the final expiry of the naval limitation treaties. They were designed as specialized attack boats with a heavy torpedo armament of eight bow tubes, plus two 25mm (0.9 in) AA guns as well as a 140mm (5.5 in) deck gun. In addition to this formidable array of conventional armament, they could also carry a Type A midget submarine, mounted "piggy back" to the aft of the conning-tower. The 1-16s had two diesel engines.

S class (*1939, Britain*)

Britain's S class boats rank among the most successful submarines ever built for the Royal Navy. A first batch of 12 was built during 1931-1938, and a vastly improved second group, 50 in all, was completed between 1942 and 1945. The most notable feature of the later S class was the all-welded hull construction for greater strength. The first S class boats suffered very heavy losses in the first year of the war, with seven of the original 12 sunk. For the first group, displacement was 681 tonnes (670 tons) and a crew of 38, with 726 tonnes (715 tons) and a crew of 44 in the second batch. The armament was six bow torpedo tubes, a 76mm (3 in) deck gun, and a machine gun for AA work. Earlier boats of the second batch were given an external stern torpedo tube.

Type VIIC (*1939, Germany*)

The Type VII ocean-going submarine formed the backbone of Germany's U-boat fleet in the Second World War. Out of the 1,162 U-boats of all classes commissioned in 1939-45, 715 were Type VIIs and most of them were Type VIICs. The Type VIIC had a displacement of 781 tonnes (769 tons) and a crew of 44. Her two-shaft diesels gave an excellent operational radius of 10,460km (6,500 miles) at 12 knots. The armament consisted of four bow and one stern 53.3cm (21 in) torpedo tubes, and an 89mm (3.5 in) deck gun. Mines could be carried instead of torpedoes. The basic AA armament was one 30mm (1.2 in) and two 20mm (0.8 in) guns, but as the Allied air threat grew some boats were fitted with two quadruple 10mm (0.4 in) mountings in addition to the 30mm (1.2 in) gun.

1-15 class (*1939, Japan*)

Also known as Type BI, these were big submarines intended to fulfil the cruiser role so mistakenly started by the French with *Surcouf*. They carried a folding seaplane in a hangar, the seaplane being launched

Type VIIC

from a catapult ramp on the foredeck. The 1-15s displaced 2,233 tonnes (2,198 tons) and had a crew of 100. The armament consisted of six bow torpedo tubes, a 140mm (5.5 in) gun, and two 25mm (1 in) anti-aircraft guns. The surface speed was high – an estimated 24 knots. But losses were great, and only one survived at the time of the surrender.

Type IX (*1939, Germany*)

Seven Type IXs had been completed by the outbreak of World War Two. They were designed as long-range ocean-going submarines, the Type IXB having nearly double the radius 17,700km (11,000 miles) of the Type VIIC, and two stern torpedo tubes to the Type VIIC's one.

Gato class (*1941, USA*)

These superb fighting machines, 195 of which were built, were designed as attack submarines, built for hitting power as well as endurance on patrol. Their displacement was 1,549 tonnes (1,525 tons) and the crew of 80 was accommodated in a hull 95m (312 ft) long. Their top surface speed was 20 to 24 knots. The armament consisted of six bow and four stern torpedo tubes, a 127mm (5 in) deck gun, and a 40mm (1.6 in) gun. Their destruction of the Japanese merchant fleet was unmatched by any other submarine navy of World War Two. The Gato class was powered by diesel/electric engines using four generators to supply the two main motors.

Type IX

Gato class

Type XVIII (*1944, Germany*)

This followed the smaller coastal Type XVII, and was intended to be the ocean-going variant. Type XVII and Type XVIII were designed to carry the revolutionary Walter turbine, with auxiliary diesel/electric drive on the center of three shafts. Walter's system used a peroxide concentrate to break down water into high-pressure gas capable of driving a turbine, producing phenomenal bursts of submerged speed in the region of 24 knots. If the U-boat offensive had been reopened in 1945 this could have yielded startling results. On the other hand, the peroxide fuel was notoriously unstable and highly dangerous, and could well have led to many accidental losses.

Type XXIII (*1944, Germany*)

The small coastal equivalent to the Type XXI – 236 tonnes (232 tons) displacement, two bow tubes and complement of 14, but the same basic power plant and silent "creeping" electric motors.

Type XXI (*1944, Germany*)

Fortunately for the Allies, Germany was overrun and the Second World War ended before these formidable submarines could re-open the Battle of the Atlantic. They were in fact the first true submarines, designed for continuous submerged patrols using the *schnorchel* or air-breathing "snort" instead of surfacing to re-charge batteries. To out-pace the Allied escorts, the Type XXI was also designed to be faster submerged (16 knots) than surfaced. Its 1,638 tonne (1,612 ton) hull housed additional battery stowage to give this high submerged speed, plus very quiet "creeping" electric motors to enhance survivability. They were armed with six bow torpedo tubes and were designed to carry four 30mm (1.2 in) guns, though the usual gun armament consisted of two twin 20mm (0.8 in) mounts. The crew was 57.

1-400 class (*1945, Japan*)

In 1945, the Japanese, with their ill-founded submarine strategy, developed the monstrous 1-400 class of submarine. Unfortunately, they proved to be as useless as their French predecessor *Surcouf* had been. The 1-400s were supposed to combine all scouting and attack roles – a hopeless contradiction in terms. Their huge hangars could accommodate three bomb-carrying seaplanes, catapulting launched from the foredeck ramp. Their conventional armament consisted of eight bow torpedo tubes, a 140mm (5.5 in) gun, and ten 25mm (1 in) AA guns. Technically, the 1-400s were indeed impressive, able to dive to 99m (325 ft), and cruise 60,350km (37,500 miles) surfaced at 14 knots. Their displacement was 5,306 tonnes (5,223 tons) and their crew exceeded 100. Only three out of an intended eighteen of this class were ever completed.

Pickerel (*1944-1950 USA*)

Launched in December 1944, *Pickerel* belonged to the late Second World War Tench class. She was one of the 15 boats of the class selected for GUPPY III conversion, being sliced in two to accommodate a 4.6m (15 ft) engine-room section. She was also given a lengthened, better streamlined "sail" type conning-tower and the ability to dive to 100 fathoms (183m (600 ft)). Returned to service during the Korean War, *Pickerel* made the 8,530-km (5,300-mile) run from Hong Kong to Pearl Harbor in 21 days without surfacing (1950). She had a crew of 80-90.

1-400 class

Tang class (*1952, USA*)

The six Tangs were the first high-speed attack submarines built for the US Navy after the end of the Pacific War and the first "Guppy" experiments of the late 1940s. They embodied many of the features of the German Type XXIs of 1944-45, such as streamlining, powerful electric motors, high submerged speeds and the ability to dive deep. Apart from the abandonment of the deck gun, a notable break with previous design tradition was a shortening of the hull, to make for greater maneuverability submerged. Displacement was 2,133 tonnes (2,100 tons), with a crew of 83; the armament was six bow and two stern torpedo tubes. Four of the class were "Guppied" in 1957 to take more powerful diesels in an additional 2.7m (9 ft) section; *Tang* underwent a second "Guppying" in 1967, when an extra 4.6m (15 ft) hull section was added.

Whisky class (*1950, USSR*)

The construction of 276 submarines of the Whisky class between 1950 and 1959 laid the foundation of the USSR's modern ocean-going navy. Though their design was not based on the most modern German U-boats assessed by the USSR after 1945, it was strongly influenced by them. The Whisky class boats were clearly imitations of the trends set by the Type XXIs and the postwar US Tangs. They were streamlined attack submarines without a deck gun. Displacement was 1,046 tonnes (1,030 tons), with a crew of 60. Their armament consisted of four bow and two stern torpedo tubes; 40 mines could be carried instead of torpedoes. After they had been supplanted as the main attack submarine class by more modern types, some Whisky class boats were fitted with mountings for the launching of Cruise missiles ("Whisky Twin Cylinder" and "Whisky Long Bin" in Western terminology). The class is in service in several navies.

Whisky class

Porpoise class (*1958, Britain*)

After 1945, British submarine development lost its way in the first ten years of peace, largely wasted in the hope of adopting the highly dangerous peroxide turbine as an alternative to nuclear power. The Porpoise class eventually emerged as a high-performance diesel/electric, able to make continuous submerged patrols anywhere in the world. The most distinctive feature of the class (as of the 13 Oberons which followed the eight Porpoises) was the sonar dome in the upper bow. Displacement was 1,630 tonnes (1,605 tons), with a crew of 71. The armament consisted of six torpedo tubes mounted in the bow and two mounted astern.

Barbel class (*1959, USA*)

Ordered in 1956, the three Barbel submarines were the last diesel/electric attack submarines built for the US Navy and may be taken as the ultimate in non-nuclear submarine design. They have the fully streamlined, "teardrop" hull shape proven by the experimental *Albacore* of 1953, the first submarine to exceed 30 knots submerged. The Barbels have a displacement of 2,184 tonnes (2,150 tons) and a crew of 77; their armament consists of six bow torpedo tubes.

Porpoise class

Nautilus

NUCLEAR ATTACK SUBMARINES – SSN

Nautilus (1955, USA)
The world's first nuclear-powered submarine sent the historic signal "UNDERWAY ON NUCLEAR POWER" on January 17, 1955. *Nautilus* was a prudent, "belt and braces" design, with three engine-room levels: nuclear, diesel and electric. Her displacement was 3,824 tonnes (3,764 tons), and she had a crew of 105 men. The armament consisted of six bow torpedo tubes. On her first reactor core, *Nautilus* steamed 111,260km (69,138 miles) and with her second core she covered 149,664km (93,000 miles) (1957-59). Of these a further 126,950km (78,885 miles) were submerged, including the first submerged crossing of the North Pole under the Arctic ice on August 3, 1958. *Nautilus* could make 20 knots on the surface and 23 knots submerged.

Skipjack (1959, USA)
Skipjack and her five sister ships were the first US SSNs with the "teardrop" hull, complete hull streamlining with sail-mounted hydroplanes, and single-shaft propulsion. The displacement is 3,124 tonnes (3,075 tons), with a crew of 93; and she carries six bow torpedo tubes. Ordered in 1956 and completed in 1959-61, the Skipjack class can make 20 knots on the surface and 35 knots submerged.

Tullibee (1960, USA)
Tullibee was the first purpose-built nuclear hunter-killer SSN, designed specifically for the anti-submarine role. With a streamlined "teardrop" hull and sail-mounted planes, she could make 15 knots surfaced and over 20 knots submerged. *Tullibee* pioneered beam-mounted torpedo-tubes in hunter-killers, permitting full and effective concentration of sonor and HE sensors in the bow.

Dreadnought (1963, Britain)
Thanks to the time wasted with research on the problem of the peroxide turbine power plant, the Royal Navy would not have acquired its first SSN so early without the "special relationship" between Britain and the USA. A special agreement signed in 1958, enabled the British to buy a complete set of propulsion equipment designed for the Skipjack class, cutting out the delay which would have been caused by the development of an all-British nuclear reactor for submarines. The result was *Dreadnought*, designed as the Royal Navy's first high-speed "hunter-killer." Though closely modeled on the Skipjack class, the conservatism of British submarine design retained hull-mounted instead of sail-mounted hydroplanes. *Dreadnought*'s displacement was 3,048 tonnes (3,000 tons), with a crew of 88 and armament of six bow torpedo tubes.

November class (1958, USSR)
The 13 Novembers were the first Soviet SSNs, completed between 1958 and 1963. They have an enormous hull length compared with their contemporaries, the US Skipjack class: 109.7m (359.8 ft) as against 76.8m (252 ft). Their two-shaft propulsion permitted four stern torpedo tubes as well as the eight in the bow, but inevitably it made for a "noisier" submarine, not helped by the large number of flooding holes in the casing. Displacement is given as 4,267 tonnes (4,200 tons).

Dreadnought

Conquerer (*1971, Britain*)
HMS *Conqueror* is the first and only SSN ever to have carried out an attack, when she sank the Argentine cruiser *General Belgrano* on May 2 1982, at the outset of the Falklands War. *Conqueror* was the second of the three Churchill class SSNs, which followed the two Valiants (1966-67) in 1970. The Churchills have a displacement of 4,470 tonnes (4,400 tons) and a crew of 103. They are armed with six bow torpedo tubes, and their announced submerged speed is 28 knots.

Conqueror

Los Angeles class (*1976, USA*)
This is the latest class of American SSN, designed for high speed and great quietness. The Los Angeles class SSNs have retained the distinctive beam-mounted torpedo tubes (leaving the bow devoted completely to sonar) established with the experimental SSN *Tullibee* of 1960. This was adopted for the 13 Thresher class SSNs (1962-67) and the 37 Sturgeons (1967-75). Displacement for the Los Angeles class is 6,096 tonnes (6,000 tons) and the crew is 127. The four midship tubes are designed for firing Harpoon air/surface missiles as well as Subroc and hunting torpedoes

against enemy submarines. The Los Angeles class has been limited by cost, the greatest ever for SSNs. Within five years the original estimate of $221.25 million per submarine had soared to $809.6 million, a price considered too great in many quarters.

Alfa class (*1980, USSR*)
The use of titanium alloy construction in this class, which has been in slow series production since the first of the class was completed in 1970, has resulted in an SSN of startling performance. It is estimated

that the titanium hull allows this class of submarine to attain diving depths in excess of 753m (2,470 ft) – a considerable improvement over previous Soviet SSN performances. The Alfas are completely different from the clumsy copies of American types represented by the first Soviet nuclear submarines. They have a speed of 42 knots submerged. It is doubtful whether the very best of NATO's anti-submarine weapons could be certain of scoring a kill in contention with such speed and depth.

Los Angeles class

Zulu class

NUCLEAR BALLISTIC MISSILE – SSBN

Zulu class (*1955, USSR*)
Though not nuclear-powered, the 28 Zulus were the first large patrol submarines built for the USSR's Navy after 1945, and six were converted as Zulu 5s to launch ballistic missiles. The sail mounting was lengthened aft to accommodate two launch tubes for the SS-N-4 Sark missile. Despite its nuclear warhead, Sark had a shorter range than the wartime German V-2 – (595km (370 miles)) – and it also had to be fired on the surface. The displacement for the Zulu class was given as, 1,981 tonnes (1,950 tons), and each boat had a crew of 75.

George Washington class
(*1959, USA*)
The US Navy was only briefly interested with Cruise missile submarines, producing only two (*Grayback* and *Growler*) in 1958 to evaluate the use of the Regulus missile. Long before Regulus was finally scrapped in 1964, the US Navy had decided to concentrate on SSBN development, with the five George Washingtons as the first generation. They displace 6,115 tonnes (6,019 tons) and have a crew of 112; each submarine has two crews, to permit rapid turn-a-round between patrols and keep as many SSBNs as possible constantly on patrol. The speeds are

20 knots surfaced and 31 knots submerged, and the SLBM carried is the Polaris A-3. Like all modern SSBNs, the George Washingtons carry bow torpedoes with 6 tubes.

Hotel class (*1958-1962, USSR*)
Built at the same time as the 19 diesel/electric Golfs, the eight Hotels also carried their three SLBM tubes in a lengthened sail structure, while carrying both bow and stern torpedo tubes. Though they were the first Soviet SSBNs, the Hotels were completely outclassed by the contemporary American George Washingtons, being both slower and noisier. Apart from this, the Golfs and Hotels together, 27 submarines

all told, only carried one more missile than the 80 carried by the five George Washingtons.

Lafayette class (*1963, USA*)
The Lafayette class consists of thirty-one ballistic missile submarines. They were originally built with sixteen missile tubes, but this was increased to twenty-four when the class was converted to accommodate the Poseidon missile. In addition, there are four bow torpedo tubes. The *James Madison* was the first of the class converted to Poseidon, in June 1970. The nuclear engine with two geared turbines gives a submerged speed in excess of 30 knots. The crew complement of the Lafayette class is 140.

Resolution class (*1967, Britain*)
After the December 1962 Nassau Agreement, in which the USA agreed to supply Britain with Polaris SLBMs, five British-built SSBNs were ordered for the Royal Navy. This was then cut down to four by the incoming Labour Government, making it impossible to keep more than one SSBN constantly on patrol. Like the US George Washingtons, the British Resolutions carry 16 Polaris A-3 missiles. Their displacement is 7,620 tonnes (7,500 tons), with a crew of 143, and a torpedo armament of six bow tubes.

Resolution class

Ohio class

Redoutable class (*1971, France*)
The French Government not only made the courageous decision to build a five-ship SSBN fleet, but did it without grossly reducing the strength of the French surface fleet (as was the Royal Navy's fate in Britain). The five Redoutables were completed between 1971 and 1980 and are armed with French-built SLBMs: currently the MSBS M-20, in 16 tubes. The displacement is 7,620 tonnes (7,500 tons) and the crew 135, with four bow torpedo tubes. The Redoutables follow the US practice of carrying their hydroplanes in the sail.

Delta class (*1972, USSR*)
The first USSR SSBNs on the lines of the George Washington class were the 34 Yankees, completed between 1967 and 1976. Their successors were the Delta class submarines, designed to carry the superior SS-N-8 SLBM. The 18 Delta Is, built between 1972 and 1977, only carried 12 SLBM tubes, but the later four Delta IIs carry 16. The latest variant is the Delta III (13 SSBNs) which carries 16 tubes for the SS-N-

18. This missile carried the USSR's SSBN fleet into the 6,440km (4,000 mile) range bracket, roughly equivalent to that of the USA's Trident SLBM. Delta II and Delta III displace 9,500 tonnes (9,350 tons), with a crew of 132. They carry six bow torpedo tubes.

Ohio class (*1981, USA*)
Though constructed earlier, the 16-tube submarines of the US SSBN fleet have been converted to carry the multi-warhead Trident missile –

the Ohio class was an entirely new concept. The missile battery has been raised from 16 tubes to 24, pushing the displacement up to 16,865 tonnes (16,600 tons). Its reported horsepower is 60,000 and the crew is 133. The bow torpedo armament consists of four tubes. All indications are that the class will, like the Los Angeles SSNs, be cut short by the staggering cost; Congress refused to authorize the $911.9 million estimated for SSBN 733, the seventh unit of the class.

Delta class

Submarines in Service Today

Number of Submarines in Service given by class

Country	Diesel/Electric submarine (SS)	Nuclear-powered attack submarine (SSN)	Diesel/Electric Ballistic submarine (SSB)	Nuclear-powered Ballistic submarine (SSBN)	Diesel/Electric Cruise missile submarine (SSG)	Nuclear-powered Cruise missile submarine (SSGN)
Argentina	Salta (3)					
Australia	Ran Oberon (6)					
Brazil	Oberon; Guppy II Type; Guppy III Type (37)					
Bulgaria	Whisky: Romeo (2)					
Canada	Oberon (3)					
China	Ming; S-1; Romeo; Whisky (107)	Han (2)	Golf (1)			
Colombia	Type 209; SX-506 (4)					
Cuba	Foxtrot; Whisky (3)					
Denmark	Narhvalen; Delfinen (4)					
Egypt	Romeo; Whisky (4)					
France	Agosta; Daphne; Arethuse (17)	SNA 72 (2)		Inflexible (1); Le Redoutable (5)		
Germany	Type 206; Type 205 (25)					
Greece	Glavkos (11)					
Israel	Type 206 (3)					
Italy	Sauro; Toti; Tang; Guppy III (12)					
Japan	Yuushio; Uzushio; Asashio (14)					
Netherlands	Walrus; Zwaardvis; Potvis (6)					
Norway	Type 207 (15)					
Pakistan	Agosta; Daphne (6)					
South Africa	Daphne (3)					
USSR	Tango; Bravo; Foxtrot; Zulu IV; Romeo; Whisky; Whisky Canvas Bag; India (228)	Alfa; Yankee; Victor III; Victor II; Victor I; Echo I; November; Mike; Sierra (76)	Golf II; Golf III; Golf V (19)	Delta III; Delta II; Delta I; Yankee; Hotel III; Hotel II Typhoon (65)	Juliett; Papa; Whisky Long Bin; Whisky; (18)	Oscar; Papa; Charlie II; Charlie I; Echo II (50)
Spain	Agosta; Daphne; S-30 (9)					
Sweden	Nacken; Sjoormen; Draken (9)					
Turkey	Type 209; Guppy III; Guppy IIA (16)					
United Kingdom	Oberon; Porpoise (15)	Trafalgar; Swiftsure; Valiant; Churchill (12)		Resolution (4)		
United States	Barbel; Darter; (4)	Los Angeles; Narwhal; Sturgeon; Thresher; Tullibee; Skipjack; Halibut; Seawolf; Ethan Allen; George Washington (95)		Ohio; Benjamin Franklin; Lafayette (43)		

All figures given are approximate.

Glossary

Acoustic mine Mine detonated by a submarine's own noises or other hydrophonic effects (HE).

Acoustic torpedo Torpedo guided to target by target's HE.

Active sonar Sonar transmitting sonic "ping" to detect submerged submarines.

ASW Anti-Submarine Warfare.

Ballast tanks The tanks which submerge the submarine when flooded, and return it to the surface when blown empty by compressed air.

Ballistic missiles Missiles which descend on the target accelerated by the downward plunge from a high trajectory.

Bow cap The streamlined outer door of a torpedo tube.

Celestial navigation Determination of ship's position from observation of sun, moon, or stars.

Coastal navigation Determination of ship's position by observing shore landmarks.

Complement The correct term for a ship's crew (officers and ratings).

COMSAT Communications Satellite.

Core The mass of radioactive material, changed when exhausted, which fuels a nuclear reactor.

Cruise missiles Missiles (non-ballistic) which fly low to their target, avoiding the enemy's radar defenses.

Dead reckoning (DR) Navigation technique using assumed positions, based on effects of course, speed, wind, tides, etc, since last accurate fix.

Depth charge A pressure-detonated "water bomb," dropped or fired by surface warships, to destroy submarines.

"Dunking" Helicopter ASW search technique, lowering sonar buoys into the sea to cover the widest possible area quickly.

Electronic Countermeasures (ECM) Usually the "jamming" of enemy signals and sensors.

ELF Extremely Low Frequency radio transmitter.

Fix An accurate plot of the ship's position.

Greater Underwater Propulsive Power (GUPP) A project in which diesel/electric submarines were cut in half to accommodate more powerful engines, then reassembled.

Hydrophonic Effects (HE) Noises from a ship or submarine detected by hydrophone.

Hydrophone A sensor which detects underwater sounds.

Hydroplanes Pitch controls which, like an aircraft's elevators, angle a submarine up or down.

ICBM Inter-Continental Ballistic Missile (land-based).

Magnetic Anomaly Detector (MAD) An ASW device carried by patrol aircraft, to detect the mass of a submerged submarine.

Multiple Independently targetable Re-entry Vehicle (MIRV) The correct term for a multi-warhead strategic missile, such as Poseidon or Trident.

Negative buoyancy A submarine's tendency to sink, imparted by flooding the ballast tanks.

Passive sonar Non-transmitting sonar which detects HE or enemy sonar transmissions.

Periscope A viewing tube with parallel mirrors, lowered when not in use, which gives an all-round view of sea and sky from a submerged submarine.

Pressure hull The reinforced main hull of a submarine, sheathed by the outer ballast tanks, designed to resist water pressure when the vessel is submerged.

Radar (Radio Direction and Ranging) A rotating electronic beam which detects ships, aircraft and coastlines in bad visibility or by night.

Running Fix A fix used in coastal navigation when only one shore landmark is visible.

Sail The streamlined tower from which a submarine is controlled or "conned" when on the surface. Formerly known as the conning tower. Also called the fin.

"Scrubber" Apparatus for removing impurities from air in a submerged submarine.

Sensor Apparatus, usually electronic, for extending the natural senses of sight and hearing, such as sonar, radar, and hydrophones.

SLBM Submarine-Launched Ballistic Missile.

"Snort" (or "Snorkel") An air-breathing tube for ventilating diesel engines when running submerged.

SS A diesel/electric submarine.

SSBN A nuclear-powered ballistic missile submarine.

SSG A diesel/electric Cruise missile submarine.

SSGN A nuclear-powered Cruise missile submarine.

SSN A nuclear-powered attack submarine.

Trim The stable condition of a submerged submarine at the depth required.

Trim tanks Small tanks to assist maintenance of the trim when water is pumped to and fro between them.

Vents Valves on top of the ballast tanks, opened to dive and closed to ascend.

Index